D0455669

# A Sacred Primer

# *A*
# *Sacred Primer*

*The Essential Guide to Quiet
Time and Prayer*

ELIZABETH HARPER NEELD, Ph.D.

RENAISSANCE BOOKS
*Los Angeles*

Library of Congress Cataloging-in-Publication Data
Neeld, Elizabeth Harper.
    A sacred primer / Elizabeth Harper Neeld.
       p.  cm.
    Includes bibliographical references and index.
    ISBN 1-58063-059-6 (alk. paper)
    1. Spiritual life.  I. Title.
    BL624.N43   1999
    291.4'4—dc21                     98-50355
                                                 CIP

10 9 8 7 6 5 4 3 2 1

*Design by Lisa-Theresa Lenthall*
*Typesetting by Jesus Arellano*

Distributed by St. Martin's Press
Manufactured in the United States of America
First Edition

*To Mahalia Jackson,*
*whose songs were my prayers long before I knew I was praying*
*and to Dr. Betty Miller Unterberger,*
*who taught me about quiet time and prayer*

# CONTENTS

*Part Four*

# ACKNOWLEDGMENTS

If words were a river, the language that flowed in my family for hundreds of years before I was born included these spiritual assertions: a powerful connection exists between human beings and God and any individual can choose to participate and grow in this intimate relationship.

I, therefore, owe tremendous debts. To my great-grandfather Plummer, who, as a twelve-year-old stowaway, slipped off the boat and into Georgia where he later became a fervent Methodist layman who in the mid and late 1800s never saw a Sunday service or a camp meeting he didn't enjoy. To my Grandma Willie who, swinging her little black pocketbook and wearing her little black hat, headed off across the pasture to go to prayer meeting at church every Wednesday night, climbing the stile and crossing through the pine thicket, taking me with her when I came to visit in the summer. To my Granddaddy Jim who always had his Bible nearby when he wasn't in the field plowing and who walked to the country church every Saturday to clean the building in preparation for Sunday services. To my father whose faith and trust in God—as a man and as a minister—never wavered, no matter what. Although she wrote the song about her own grandfather, I always imagined Dolly Parton included Tommie Harper when she sang, "Daddy was an Old-Time Preacher-Man." To my mother, Rachel Harper, about whom the writer in the Epistle to the Hebrews in the New Testament could easily have been referring when he wrote, "Be careful, for you may be entertaining angels unawares." Rachel did not only love; she *was* love. To my Aunt Frances who carries that love forward now. To my sister, Barbara, and my brother, Frank, who along with me are the fortunate beneficiaries of the spiritual conversations we inherited, which we carry on today in whatever way we are able.

Every author knows the gap that exists between having something to say and finally being able to write this in a way that stands even a chance of contributing to others. Many people have joined to help me span that gap. Joe McNeely, my editor at Renaissance Books, who guides and checks; and, in so doing, becomes a valued collaborator. Robin Cantor Cook, who offers an editorial reading eye honed by years of experience. Kimbria Hays and Cathy Baehler, who copyedit with a professional, thorough touch. Lisa Lenthall provided the elegant design, and Michael Dougherty continues to work to see that people have a chance to know about *A Sacred Primer*. A special thank you to Ben Whitehouse, whose oil painting *Path to the Lake* graces the cover and to my editor for serendipitously discovering this wonderful artist during a rain storm in Chicago.

Friends and colleagues, coming from many professions and with myriad thoughts and experiences of their own, patiently critiqued chapter by chapter as I wrote the first draft: Faye Walker, Linda Chamberlain, Christine Reel, Barbara Walker, Kathi Appelt, Kathy Reiter, David Kaplan, Nancy Sears, Frank Harper,

Eva Archer-Smith, Irma Starr, Lee Herrick, Pippa Wiley, Sheri Harper. Other readers responded to a completed draft and on very short notice: Paula Wong, Anne Bustard, Pat Martin, Betty Unterberger, George-Ella Anderson-Wood. Sandi Jackson made beautiful pen-and-ink drawings when we thought *A Sacred Primer* would be an illustrated book. Karen McCarver, Taniel Lepla, and Colleen O'Grady shared experiences from their sacred quiet times. Eleven executives, artists, and professionals generously contributed the pieces in the book called "An Inspirational Voice."

Almost ten years ago my agent, Chris Tomasino, told me how much she enjoyed my writing and how much she believed in my work. I deeply appreciate her commitment to me and my books.

Sharing life with my husband Jerele Neeld makes everything I do more meaningful, and I am deeply grateful.

# INTRODUCTION

Why would someone who has no religious occupation write a book on sacred quiet time and prayer? Someone who is a business consultant and a writer of biographies and books on subjects like life after loss? Someone whose life is crammed full of plane schedules, work assignments, family commitments, and occasionally a day or two off to relax?

I can answer these questions very simply.

I have written this book, *A Sacred Primer*, because establishing a daily spiritual practice of quiet time and prayer is the most important decision I ever made.

It began like this. . . .

At the age of thirty-nine, a tenured, full professor in liberal arts, I had gotten myself from the hills of Tennessee (and a restrictive religious upbringing) to New York City with all its personal freedom, and then on to the directorship of a graduate program in a large university and a reputation as a national leader in my academic field.

But I was also a woman whose life's structure had been blown to smithereens by the sudden death of her young husband. In the aftermath of that terrible event many questions plagued me: What matters anyway? Does anything have meaning? What is my life about? I was in a why-am-I-here full-blown crisis.

During this time of personal trauma, Dr. Betty Miller Unterberger, another professor at the university, invited me to lunch. I had never met Dr. Unterberger, but I knew she was a famous historian who was often called to Washington to consult in matters of international relations. During lunch I kept thinking, "Something about this woman is different. Sure, she's a well-known thinker and scholar; but there's something else." Near the end of lunch, she mentioned a tragedy in her own life the year before, and I sputtered, "But you are so serene. How could this have happened and you still be so peaceful?"

"For twenty-four years," she answered, "I have practiced a spiritual discipline every morning before I do anything else in my day."

Dr. Unterberger introduced a subject I knew little about. I made no distinction between a spiritual life and religion, and, at that time in my life, I considered religion stifling, threatening, and haranguing. Therefore, I paid no attention to anything to do with an inner life.

But perhaps, I thought, I am missing something. Clearly there is something my lunch companion knows and experiences that makes a visible difference.

Being a researcher and a scholar, I dove into the subject of the spiritual life in much the same way that I dove into research on Samuel Richardson's eighteenth century novels or the relationship of architecture to the writing process. I began by looking at the history of the Western spiritual traditions. (Western because that is what I am.) I asked questions: Over the ages, what were those people whom we today characterize as spiritual talking about, practicing, experiencing? What is the thread that runs through the lives of, say, the Old Testament prophets in 300 B.C., Hildegard of Bingen in the 1100s, Dame Julian of Norwich in 1373, Dietrich Bonhoeffer in Nazi Germany, the Jewish theologian Martin Buber, and Mother Teresa in the late twentieth century? What do these people share in common that we might label a spiritual life?

I never dreamed where the research that began with that chance conversation with Betty Unterberger would lead. What started as an academic investigation became, over time, a personal and passionate interest. I discovered the gift of paying attention to the spiritual life. What is that gift? Life becoming, more and more, the satisfying adventure it was meant to be. My becoming, more and more, the person I was meant to be. My daily pursuits becoming, more and more, the meaningful activities they were meant to be.

Some years ago, I left the academic world and began to do business consulting and to write books. I don't know if I would ever have found the courage to give up a tenured, full professorship if I had not begun to explore the spiritual life and discovered a source of direction, confidence, and clarity I never knew before.

It may seem like a strange thing to say, but I am a fan of the spiritual life. An enthusiastic, supportive, all-weather fan. To share the marvelous, mysterious, majestic experience of living life at the bone—an experience that comes with paying attention to what is really important—is why I have written this book that you are now reading.

# NOTE TO READERS

Among several other names—like the Divine, the Eternal, *Spiritus Creator,* and Holy Other—you will find the name, God, included in the forms of address in this book. The use of the word God raises questions for some people because of bitter memories and negative experiences. The traditional name has been subjected to most unfortunate uses in history. I choose to associate the name God, however, with images of the Divine found throughout sacred Scripture:

- a caring shepherd
- an eagle carrying us on its wings
- a woman searching for a lost coin and, upon finding it, calling in the community to celebrate
- a light
- a hen protecting her young
- sweet water gushing from a rock
- oil of gladness
- a potter lovingly remaking a pot that is flawed

- a woman in labor giving birth
- a sheltering rock
- a father forgiving his son and throwing a big party
- clear heat in summer and a cloud of dew in the heat of harvest

The name, God, certainly does not refer to a white-haired man who lives on a throne somewhere above the clouds. God, when used here, means the Highest; the creative, most-powerful Creator of the universe; the supreme ground of love who is as near to us as the breath we breathe.

Why use the word at all? There's a story told about Jewish theologian Martin Buber that helps me answer this question. Buber was visiting in the home of a philosopher who asked him one morning to read aloud what Buber was proofreading. The host, upon hearing the material read, reacted vehemently. He asked Buber how he could bring himself to say "God" time after time when so much injustice had been done in that name. Buber replied, "Yes, it is the most heavy-laden of all human words. None has become so soiled, so mutilated. Just for this reason I may not abandon it. . . . We cannot cleanse the word God and we cannot make it whole; but defiled and mutilated as it is, we can raise it from the ground and set it over an hour of great care."

It is my desire, with Professor Buber, to raise the name of God and "set it over an hour of great care"; to associate the name of God rightly, with Holy Being, Love, and Caring Presence.

*They that wait upon the Lord shall renew their strength.*
*They shall mount up with wings like eagles.*
*They shall run and not be weary. They shall walk and not faint.*

—Isaiah 40:31

*Part One*

&#x2042;

# REMEMBERING SACRED MOMENTS

*There are those two or three images in whose presence our hearts were first opened; we spend the rest of our lives returning to those images.*

—*William Auden*

We have all had those moments that felt sacred. We all remember them. Some deep, timeless part of us was touched. What is beyond became present. It was as if the Eternal, ever so fleetingly, broke through to the earthly. A new dimension became present in our human life.

But, for most of us, the gap seems huge between remembering those moments when the Divine broke through and dealing with the pressures and demands of everyday life. How can I be thinking about the spiritual in the middle of a traffic jam or when the kids skip school or when the boss expects the work of two employees for the price of one? Now that is another matter.

We are inspired by reading and discussing spiritual matters; we make resolutions about remembering, and acting on spiritual principles. We want life to have meaning and purpose. But our good intentions evaporate as we rush out the door late for work, or hunt for the time to help make a mask of a president for fourth grade social studies, or hurriedly thaw last week's casse-role hoping everybody will think it's fresh.

To learn how to invite the Divine into our daily lives is the focus of this book. To explore how we who work in the mar-ketplace, cook spaghetti for the family, go to school, balance the checkbook, and cut the grass can practice the spiritual life. How we can experience the Eternal, not only in special, fleet-ing moments but as a daily presence. How we can bridge the gap between reading and thinking about—even longing for—a fuller spiritual life and practicing this life in such a way that we have more peace, take care of our souls, and experience bal-ance and equilibrium, even during the windstorms of our lives.

Perhaps you have intended to add a daily spiritual practice to your life for years now. You recognize it is time to design and create a structure to support you in this intention. That is what we, in the rest of this book, will do together.

## CHILDHOOD MEMORIES

I suspect we keep returning to these moments when our hearts were first opened because they were experiences of meaning and connection. They have become the lodestars of our personal internal universe. In the memory of these images, we experience a reality beyond the mundane.

For many of us, the transcendent moment when our hearts were first opened occurred when we were children. Perhaps we were sitting with our friends around a campfire under a canopy of bright stars, singing simple melodies. Perhaps we were run-ning through the grass, or attending a funeral, or celebrating a religious ritual. Perhaps we were standing at a window, looking out at the shimmering heat or rain falling on the pavement. Per-haps our grandmother was in the kitchen singing.

Dr. Robert Coles from Harvard whose engaging book, *The Spiritual Life of Children,* records dozens of first-hand accounts, suggests that such spiritual moments are normal, frequent, and ubiquitous for children. I have found, in talking to adults about their spiritual memories, that the impact of these early experiences is also long-lasting. One woman in her late seventies told me about a moment—she could not have been more than five, she said—when she was enveloped with a rush of love after saying her nightly prayer. She described the color of the bedspread, the way the light from outside played on the wall: The image in which the heart is first opened. "It was such a sweet moment," she told me. "I knew from then on that it was a wonderful thing to pray."

As I survey my own past, an experience that occurred when I was a preschooler stands out as the first time I experienced a conscious connection to the Divine. It was a warm August night in South Georgia. The conversation was about seeing and being seen. And it was about love.

The soil was sandy with patches of grass where sunlight managed to slip through the dense branches of tall, skinny pine trees. Rubber-soled Sunday shoes crunched on the sand. Voices rose and fell with the familiar rhythms of friendly talk.

I, an always-moving four-year-old, entertained myself while the adults conversed by swinging left to right, right to left, holding onto my father's knee. While I swung this way, then that way, I held my head back so far I could look up through the dark night, past the fans of pine needles, to the bright, bright moon overhead.

I chanted aloud as I swung.

*I see the moon. The moon sees me.*
*God bless the moon. And God bless me.*

There were three people in my private conversation that Sunday night. Me. (A four-year-old, naturally, comes first.) The moon. And God.

The moon and I were paying attention to each other. I noticed her. She noticed me. (The moon has always been a woman for me—a fat mama sometimes, a sultry silver dancer sometimes, other shapes in between.)

Then there was God. Some power different from both the moon and me. Approachable. Available. Generous to listen and generous to bless. I wanted the moon blessed, as well as myself. I was speaking to a God who would see and bless us both.

This, I realize today, was my first spontaneous conversation with the Divine. I have no memory of learning the rhyme, although I suspect my Grandmother Margie taught it to me. But I have such a vivid memory of this particular scene that it has followed me my entire life. I can still hear the sand under my white leather Sunday high tops, feel the delicious dizziness of swinging on my father's knee, remember the sense that I was really having a conversation with God: The image in which the heart is first opened.

## A TRANSFORMING MOMENT

For others of us, the memory of connecting with something outside ourselves happened when we were adult, perhaps when we were in dire circumstances. My husband had such an experience on a small boat while crossing open seas. A friend who had been an educator took his retirement savings and bought a thirty-three-foot craft that had long ago seen its better days. He asked Jerele, who had never been on a sailboat, to be mate for an overnight passage across ocean waters. They would leave the Caribbean harbor of St. Kitts-Nevis at sunup and dock around daybreak the next day at Tortola in the British Virgin Islands.

A storm blew all day, bringing thirty-knot winds and fifteen-foot waves breaking over the side of the boat. Both men became seasick. But the worst was to come. Doing ship-watching duty shortly after midnight, Jerele announced he could see both starboard and port lights, which meant a vessel was moving straight toward them. There was no way to make contact. Either their small craft would be spotted on the approaching ship's radar, or they would be struck.

Jerele reported that the next few minutes were among the most clarifying of his life. Distinctions became crystal clear: What brought meaning and purpose to his life; what did not. What mattered; what did not. Where his allegiance belonged; where it did not. Where he got fulfillment; where he did not.

The approaching vessel—a Norwegian cruise liner—did finally spot the small sailboat and turned to avoid the collision. But the experience for Jerele was no midnight conversion, to be forgotten in the morning. Major changes occurred over the months following his return home. He deepened his commitment to a daily spiritual practice. He started teaching a Sunday School class for eleven-year-olds, even taking our new pound puppy, Dusty, to class one day to use in a lesson on caring for others. And he initiated the process that eventually resulted in his leaving a successful business which he had created and owned to work in a different field in a position that he felt was truer to his life's purpose. Ten minutes on a boat in dangerous seas: An image in which the heart is opened.

## AN EXPERIENCE OF JOY

Still another type of experience may have brought the Divine into an ordinary day—an experience of quiet (or maybe wild!) joy. Perhaps you were deeply moved by an experience that resulted in a feeling of awe and wonder. Perhaps you revved with new energy, soared in exhilaration. I remember a moment of awe and mystery the first time I held my niece, Amanda. She was only days old. My husband and I had flown from Texas to California just to see her.

There was the white crib trimmed in crisp ruffles, the small white pillow with its simple white-on-white embroidered case, the light coming in the window. I remember reaching to get this tiny person out of her crib. She was asleep and moved ever so slightly to settle into my arms. Looking down at her sweet face, I felt the insignificance of all I could ever know and understand about human life. Here was a new person, a new little individual with her own DNA, her own combination of genes, her own version of the continuation of the families of her father and mother. New life. How marvelous, how inexplicable the way life continues. If I had to find one word today to describe that first meeting with little Amanda, I would have to say that moment of quiet joy was holy.

Verena Kast, the Swiss philosopher and writer, talks about the wild joy we human beings also fall into. "It is my opinion," she asserts, "that the entire body can beam. In true delight, the entire body beams." The source of this kind of delight is deep and unfathomable. We can only call the experience ecstasy. We are outside ourselves, beyond ourselves, existing in an eternal moment.

Many years ago I had such an experience. My young husband, Greg, dropped dead while jogging, and for a long time I did not believe I would ever enjoy life again. Then one night I had a dream that resulted in a kind of beaming in both my inner and outer life, a delight which came from somewhere outside myself. A beaming that was holy.

In the dream I was walking along a residential street. To my right was a lawn that sloped gently upward toward someone's home. On the edge of the lawn, near to the road, I saw a plant that looked as if it had been pulled up and just left there. I went to the plant. When I picked it up, I saw that the plant had roots and the roots were still alive! I became ecstatic in the dream, joyfully running along the road calling, "The plant can be planted again. The roots are alive. The roots are alive."

When I awoke the next morning, I felt enthusiastic for the first time in months. I had energy. Joy rose in me like bright colored balloons. From that moment on, I was back in the land of the living. The Divine had intervened; healing had occurred.

## A GRADUALLY INCREASING PERCEPTION

For others, recognition of a connection to the sacred increases gradually, perhaps almost imperceptibly. My mother, Rachel, was one person who could never put her finger on one defining moment when the Divine became real for her; it seemed, she said, that she had always known God.

*Even when I was just a little girl, living in Atlanta during the Depression, I would pray. My family didn't go to church at that time, but I knew that God was someone I could talk to. Once when we needed money, I convinced my parents to let my brother and me bring back buckets of pears from the country when we went to visit relatives. We had a whole bathtub full. Eliot and I went up and down the streets in our neighborhood trying to sell those pears. We didn't sell a one. But, back on the swing on the porch, I told Eliot I was going to sing a song anyway, that I knew God would help us, even if we couldn't sell the pears. So I made up a ditty about two country kids who came to the big city and were so poor they couldn't even sell pears. I taught it to Eliot and we sang it in our loudest voices.*

*I felt a source of security, felt that we human beings are cared for and loved by God even when we have to live in tough circumstances. And that security and certainty have only increased during the years.*


### SPIRITUS CREATOR BLOWING LIKE A WIND

What do these different-and-yet-similar experiences have in common: A four-year-old communicating with God as she chants "I see the moon"; Jerele, on a small boat, getting clear about his priorities; I, standing in awe and wonder as I held my new niece, Amanda, or finding, as the depressed dreamer, the plant whose roots are still alive; Rachel, my mother, experiencing a deep sense of security while she was singing her song about not being able to sell the pears?

They are all examples of an intangible yet undeniable characteristic of human life: our ability to connect with Something Other. This connecting takes us out of the ordinary and puts us into the extraordinary. The memory of this connecting becomes the source of wonder, comfort, inspiration, and direction. When the impact of the connecting moment is strong enough, we may even trace to that event the start of a journey of transformation of the very way we think about and live our lives.

This Something Other with which we connect is generative, always at work in our lives, always underlying our conscious thinking, if only we knew it. It's a thrust toward cohesion and completeness. A drive toward roundness, toward wholeness and meaning. Even when we are unaware of it, this Something Other is striving to make a solid center for us that holds, a force field around which the filings of our scattered lives can adhere and shape themselves into a meaningful pattern. Kierkegaard, the nineteenth-century philosopher, characterized our relationship to this generative Something Other—this *Spiritus Creator* he called it—as a "transparent" grounding in "the Power that posits the self."

*Spiritus Creator* has a wind-like quality; it often takes us by surprise and leads us where we would not otherwise go. The twelfth-century poet Hildegard describes the Divine:

> *I, the highest and fiery power, have kindled every living spark*
> *I have breathed out nothing that can die*
> *And by means of the airy wind, I stir everything into*
> *    quickness*
> *With a certain invisible life which sustains all . . .*

The blowing of this generative "airy wind," has enormous integrity—the integrity of nudging us toward those activities and ways of living that are right for us, that fulfill our longings and satisfy us, that use our abilities and talents. (Didn't the essayist Emerson remind us a long time ago that our talents are our calling?)

There's a wonderful example, in the book of Exodus in the Old Testament of the Bible, of *Spiritus Creator* stirring individuals in ways that use their talents and bring them personal fulfillment. The story starts with instructions which God gives Moses: "Make a sanctuary for me, that I may dwell among you. Make this tabernacle and all its furnishings exactly like the pattern I will show you."

This sanctuary and its furnishings were to be beautiful and sensuous. A chest of acacia wood overlaid with pure gold . . . a lamp stand with flower-like cups, buds and blossoms all carved of pure gold in one piece . . . ten curtains of finely twisted linen and blue, purple and scarlet yarn . . . perfume and incense made of myrrh, sweet cinnamon, oil of the olive. The writers of Exodus describe the connection between *Spiritus Creator* and human beings like this:

*Those whose hearts were stirred by God's Spirit returned with their offerings of materials for the Tabernacle, its equipment, and for the holy garments . . . Men and women came, all who were willing-hearted . . . the women skilled in sewing and spinning prepared blue, purple, and scarlet thread and cloth, and fine-twined linen and brought them in. Some of the women gladly used their special skill to spin the goats' hair into cloth. So the people of Israel—every man and woman who wanted to assist in the work given to them by the Lord's command to Moses—brought their freewill offerings.*

The writers go on to say that so many creations came in, Moses sent a message throughout the camp announcing that no more donations were needed, and those creating the sanctuary had more than enough to complete the job.

## THE MEETING OF HUMAN AND DIVINE

Someone once said that all of life is meeting. If so, there is no more important meeting in our entire lifetime than the meeting between us as human beings—who have the capacity to question and who are free to choose to take responsible action—and *Spiritus Creator* that pulls us toward an ever-receding horizon of infinite mystery and our own deepest longings for fulfillment. Martin Buber, the eminent Jewish theologian, once said that the great images of the Divine come into being not simply as a projection of our imagination but as an awakening from the deep abyss of human existence through a real encounter with divine power and glory. This encounter, this meeting, not only evokes the Divine but also brings us to birth as persons. For it is out of such encounters that we become more and more who we really are, who we really want to be.

## PERSONAL SACRED STORIES

Images that opened our hearts stay with us. They tell us what is important in our own inner life. They speak with a personal integrity that no one else can question. When we remember the sacred images and experiences that brought us insight, ecstasy, confidence, awareness, joy, and a sense of mystery and awe, we connect with a Self that recognizes an eternal relationship with the Divine. The honoring of that connection—aligning with the Holy—thousands of individuals from many cultures over hundreds of centuries have told us, is what brings contentment, satisfaction, and peace.

A few years ago I began to reconstruct my personal sacred story by listing the images and experiences that have stayed with me over the years, moments when I was blessed by an encounter, a meeting, with the Divine. The earliest was the prayer for the moon and me; but there are many others, scattered throughout my life: The first time I viewed Mesa Verde, the ancient cliff dwelling of the Anasazi, and felt glory run throughout my body. An exquisitely beautiful moment listening to the choir in church one Sunday morning and then hearing words from the minister that illumined my life. The Good Friday I joined with Greek villagers to ring the bell in their churchyard—sorrowfully, they coached, yet joyfully. The first day I was back home after my mother's funeral when the red Texas star hibiscus that grew in my backyard in Texas—and which had been a favorite of hers even though she lived far away in Tennessee—burst into bloom with not one blossom but with more than a dozen. You, too, can recall your own list of sacred moments.

The great value of reminiscence is that it tells us something did happen. Our memories are not mere abstractions but are still present and available to us as sources of awareness, learning, and wisdom; as reminders of our deepest desires; as part of the context we have for making decisions in the present. It is the aliveness of past sacred moments and the potentiality of future ones that draws us even to consider taking the time and giving the energy each day to commit to a spiritual practice.

The image in which the heart is first opened.

## R E F L E C T I O N

*In the presence of what images was your heart first opened?*

### SACRED TASKS

We all have our own sacred story: Those times when we felt a connection with *Spiritus Creator.* Images that opened our hearts. Moments when we felt moved, touched, awakened. A time that felt holy.

For six years I have met on a regular basis with a group of young mothers who want to include a spiritual practice in their daily lives. In working with these women, I have found that writing down sacred stories (even if only to make a list) provides a foundation that is personal, solid and indisputable.

TASK: Using your remembrances and your memories, create your personal sacred story. You might want to write in a journal or create a new computer file to record your sacred story. What events, moments, insights do you remember when you felt a connection with the Divine? What experiences have you had that you would call holy? These reminiscences become your own sacred autobiography, your personal sacred story.

One of the ways I use my own sacred story is to think of it as a thread that runs through my life, sometimes seen more clearly than at other times, but always weaving through the ins and outs, ups and downs, of my days. When I want or need to remind myself of why I ever first thought about committing to a daily spiritual practice, I review my sacred story. When I am in a period during which I feel nothing but despair, I remember a time I did feel a connection to God; and this memory creates at least a small possibility that I might feel such a connection again. I look back at my sacred story when the demands of my external life start to sap my spirit and remind myself that by honoring my inner life I become stronger and more able to deal with what comes to me.

TASK: Explore how your own sacred images and experiences of the past are useful today. What is the thread of continuity waiting to be picked up and brought forward? In what way can your sacred story be available as a source of wisdom; as a reminder of your deepest desires; and as part of the context for making decisions in the present?

I can tell the difference in my work day if I skip my spiritual discipline. Because I spend fifty to sixty percent of my time at work, I can easily begin to think that part of my life is of ultimate importance, getting caught up in my performance, what deal I might miss, what is happening at the office. All this is awfully enticing.

But what is of ultimate importance is another reality altogether, the reality of who I am and whose I am. I step into this other reality by spending time reading and praying and centering myself. I take this sacred time—about fifteen minutes—every morning as a discipline, just like exercising and watching what I eat. I need it every day. It is the center I look for, the place where I think seriously about my life and where I put myself in the flow of God.

I've been taught and encouraged by society to hurry, to do, to conquer. This daily quiet time was hard for me to establish because it is about not going, not doing, not conquering. But the spiritual practice has made a huge difference. I have a new perspective on my work and career. I have more confidence in what I believe and what I don't believe. I have more energy to give to people, to be with people. I've always served on boards and worked in civic activities; but now I'm called to work with people in need, such as through a prison ministry. I feel more alive and centered. My family and friends even tell me I smile more.

—J. C., executive vice president,
Fortune 500 company

# Chapter Two

### ✦

# ENCOURAGING A SPIRITUAL ATTITUDE

*Only the pure in heart can make a
good soup.*

*—Ludwig van Beethoven*

Most of us cannot just bop right into a major change that requires making time for a new activity, setting a different schedule, and committing to integrate something into our regular and ordinary life that we might have associated in the past only with holy days and the church, synagogue, or temple. "I don't have time to breathe as it is . . . and I'm considering establishing a spiritual discipline in my daily life?" we probably say to ourselves. "Whatever am I thinking?"

Indeed, whatever am I thinking?

This, I've discovered as I've worked over the years to establish my own consistent spiritual practice, is a central question. Whatever am I thinking?

I'm not talking here about positive versus negative thinking, though I certainly know the difference in the quality of my life when I choose positive over negative. I'm not talking about self-talk to help manage myself more successfully, though that kind of thinking, too, is very valuable. I'm not talking about thinking as problem-solving or thinking as idea-creation. I have learned that I must examine the very fabric of my thinking, almost the background against which I think, to see what assumptions, beliefs, and understandings determine what I do or don't do on a daily basis. I have needed to make explicit and clear to myself what, otherwise, would be the unexamined givens that determine the shape of my days.

I have done this kind of examined thinking, more often than I would like to admit, as an aftermath of failure and disappointment. But the questioning has produced some valuable results, no matter what spurred me to ask, "Whatever am I thinking?" I have learned, over the years, that certain things I think promote my ability to include sacred quiet time and prayer in my life; and I try to keep these distinctions conscious and present. I consider that these ways of thinking make up my spiritual attitude.

## THE POWER OF ATTITUDE TO ALTER OUR LIVES
Having moved to Texas from New York City, I still find myself, years after adopting the state as home, noticing things Texan. When it is time for the annual weeks of rodeo in our area, any business that can possibly do so advertises with a western flair. I was amused to see a few days ago a portable marketing sign in front of a shoe store which read, "Wear cowboy boots. It gives you an attitude."

We have all experienced the power of a new attitude to alter the context—and the actions—of our lives. This attitude, as we are more and more informed by it, becomes a way of thinking, a way of noticing, a way of paying attention that spills out to everything around us. Perhaps you reclaimed your personal power after giving it away for a long time to someone more dominating and controlling. In this case, you changed your attitude about your own value and possibility. Perhaps you started saving money, budgeting, and planning for retirement after being a spendthrift or after procrastinating for many years. In this case, you changed your attitude about your own fiscal responsibility. Perhaps, after years of thinking you would always be inept, you decided you could learn to surf the net, connect your far-flung family by e-mail, or order books through your computer. In so doing, you adopted a new attitude about technology.

How would I go about describing an attitude that can lead to a fully realized, satisfying spiritual life? What makes up that attitude? I can think of at least four things:

- Acknowledging the existence of an inner life.
- Desiring that the inner life and the outer life be aligned, and being willing to work toward this harmony.
- Choosing a method of inquiry about things spiritual that allows for new, unexpected possibilities.
- Giving committed time and attention to the spiritual dimension of life.

## A SPIRITUAL ATTITUDE: ACKNOWLEDGING THE EXISTENCE OF AN INNER LIFE

When I was ten, eleven, twelve years old, I lived a second, alternative life. This life spun itself out every night from six o'clock to six thirty while I washed the supper dishes and listened to Guy Lombardo and his band on the radio playing their "sweetest music this side of heaven." I wasn't standing alone at a scratched-up kitchen sink in a church parsonage in Rossville, Georgia. I didn't have to ride my bicycle three blocks further to reach the grocery store where a five-pound bag of sugar was ten cents cheaper. I didn't have to wear oxfords that laced instead of penny loafers.

Instead, washing dishes and listening to Lombardo's music, I was deep in a rich inner world. A world where my parents were able to buy me a dozen matching outfits at one time, red and white striped top with red skirt, blue and white top with blue skirt, yellow with yellow . . . everything to my heart's content. Then they gave me a little convertible car to go with the great clothes. I rivaled even Nancy Drew, the star of the latest book Mrs. Miller had saved for me at the public library.

Ah, the great divide between an imaginary world that gave me so much pleasure and the much starker realities of my daily life.

Somewhere along the way I started to distrust that rich, creative inner part of myself and committed everything to making good in my outer life. But the inner self was always there, neglected to be sure, but waiting. It took some shocking trauma, a lot of days of feeling dry and shriveled, and a full measure of discontent to push me to reconnect with the only part of myself that was truly vital—the inner life, which includes the imagination, but which is so much more. The spiritual life.

This spiritual life is not a "fenced-off devotional patch rather difficult to cultivate and needing to be sheltered from the outside world." To the contrary, the spiritual life is the core of who we are. It is life with a capital L. It is that part of us that loves. That longs for connection. That is unsatisfied without purpose and meaning. The part that recognizes a Reality larger than and different from human reality, that feels a part of a larger scheme of things. That experiences awe, wonder, miracle, which we may call Sacred, Holy, Divine. Our spiritual life is Life at the depth. Our depths.

I don't know of anyone who has described this inner life better than the theologian, mystic, poet, and philosopher Dr. Howard Thurman. Here is what he says about the inner life:

*As a person, each of us lives a private life; there is a world within where for us the great issues of our lives are determined. It is here that at long last the yea and nay of our living is defined, declared. It is private. It is cut off from the immediate involvement in what surrounds us. . . . Here, with the smell of life upon us, we come into the Presence of God.*

If we look at why many people have only brief bird-on-the-wing brushes with this inner life, I suspect we would have to start at the church, the temple, the parish, the religious school. For many of us, something went wrong there.

One thing that went wrong was fear. I can recall the clammy cold in my chest when the preacher talked about bad people being left behind at the day of the judgment. In the world where I grew up, God was dangerous. Watching you. Taking your name. You never knew when, in a minute, you might be wiped out. God was not someone to love. God was someone to fear. Many others have similar stories.

Perhaps it's even worse, though, for those of us who had neither good nor bad experiences at church or Sabbath School or the school assembly. We sleepwalked through religious ceremonies, passed notes to entertain ourselves through sermons, daydreamed as the chorus droned. Our depths were never touched. Our spirits were not lifted. We marked time. So we don't even have the energy of resistance.

Perhaps the place to start, then, in acknowledging an inner life is to separate this inner life from religion. They are not, of course, mutually exclusive, yet they are distinct. Today religion is alive in many places and in the hearts of many people, as a yeasty, birthing, uniting sacred activity. Hearing the Torah read, eating the bread and drinking the wine, repeating prayers that have seeded faith and knowing for hundreds of generations: these rituals speak to millions of people every week, guide their lives in meaningful ways, provide genuine succor and wisdom and rest.

But rituals carry power only when those participating in them feel a connection to the Holy. Religious activities and this sacred connection are not synonymous. Millions of others every week perform these rituals only as a duty, a habit, a badge (or perhaps as a talisman)—or know about the rituals but never desire to partake in them at all. Public communal religion, then, is not the same as having direct experiences of the Divine as part of your inner being.

To cultivate a spiritual attitude, acknowledge that you do have an inner life that is personal, that is present wherever you are present. This inner life is distinct from external religious participation, though it may certainly include it. Your inner life is the place where the very yea and nay of your life is sourced and determined. This makes the critical distinction between inner and outer life.

## A SPIRITUAL ATTITUDE: DESIRING HARMONY BETWEEN OUR INNER AND OUTER LIVES

Once I sat on the shore of the Atlantic Ocean and watched a shrimp boat with its high riggings and poles move toward the open ocean. There was a moment when the architectural lines of the boat and the natural line of the horizon met in such a beautiful configuration that I could feel the visual fit between the two. "Ah," I said, "what I am seeing is harmony."

Paul Winter, the composer and musician, found a most unexpected source of harmony when he recorded the sounds of a humpback whale, a timber wolf, and an African fish eagle for his album *Common Ground*. After he taped the animals in the wild, he discovered in the studio that the sounds of the eagle, the whale, and the wolf, while at different intervals on the scale, were all in the same key, the key of D flat. Winter tells this story on the cover of the album and comments that once a teacher told him the sound of the earth itself was D flat. Harmony . . . in more places than we may ever know.

When we turn to talk about harmony as a component of a spiritual attitude, we are talking about congruence, a fit, a pleasing agreement between our inner and outer lives. No one has described this desired harmony better, I think, than Anne Morrow Lindbergh. Writing the book, *Gift from the Sea,* Lindbergh had the opportunity to contrast her busy, complex life as the mother of five children and the wife of a world-recognized man with the quietness and calm of days spent on an isolated beach. During this time by the sea, she becomes clear about her deepest desires:

> But I want first of all—in fact, as an end to these other desires—to be at peace with myself. I want a singleness of eye, a purity of intention, a central core to my life that will enable me to carry out these obligations and activities as well as I can. I want, in fact—to borrow from the language of the saints—to live "in grace" as much of the time as possible . . . .By grace I mean an inner harmony, essentially spiritual, which can be translated into outward harmony. I am seeking perhaps what Socrates asked for in the prayer from the Phaedrus when he said, 'May the outward and inward man be at one.' I would like to achieve a state of inner spiritual grace from which I could function and give as I was meant to in the eye of God.

The inner spiritual harmony that Lindbergh is talking about occurs when the part of us that is eternal aligns with the source of all being. This source we may call God, the Eternal, Reality, a Higher Power, or something else. But whatever the name, the human finite spirit can and does connect to *Spiritus Creator.*

Anne Morrow Lindbergh worked to achieve the harmony between inner and outer life that she desired. She asserts:

> *But there are techniques of living too; there are even techniques in the search for grace. And techniques can be cultivated. I have learned by some experience, by many examples, and by the writings of countless others before me, also occupied in the search, that certain environments, certain modes of life, certain rules of conduct are more conducive to inner and outer harmony than others.*

A lovely friend of mine, now in her later years, was, as a young girl, Anne Morrow Lindbergh's secretary. She has given me a clue about what environments, modes of life and rules of conduct Lindbergh might have employed to work toward the harmony of her inner and outer life.

On most days, my friend Wren tells me, this busy woman, in spite of the tremendous demands of her life, made the time to go away from the house to a small building on the top of a rise nearby. Wren says her most vivid picture of Lindbergh, even now, more than five decades later, is seeing her set off across the yard toward this retreat site day after day, a basket, containing books, writing materials, sprigs of flowers, and whatever else she might want for this solitary quiet time, swinging on her arm. When Lindbergh returned, dinner conversation that night would often contain references to things read, ideas gleaned, thoughts stirred up in the time of solitude. There is no question in my friend's mind that Anne Morrow Lindbergh actively sought the inner and outer harmony she so desired.

But many of us, even while deeply desiring such a life of congruence between our inner and outer lives, would have to say with Charles Lamb, the English essayist of the 1800s, "Sentimentally, I am disposed to harmony; but organically I am incapable of a tune." At least, however, we can cultivate an attitude that recognizes the possibility of inner and outer harmony, a correspondence and fit with the Eternal that results in a sense of purpose and meaning to life in our everyday world, even if we know that at the present we are far from achieving it.

## A SPIRITUAL ATTITUDE:
## INQUIRING WITH OPENNESS

The spiritual life will never be centered on rock-hard, incontrovertible proof that convinces all people at all times, with nary a doubt. But then neither are mathematics, physics, medicine, nor even what are called the hard sciences centered on rock-hard, incontrovertible proof. These disciplines with all their theorems and physical laws and scientific methods never provide the last word and are always open to new breakthroughs, shifts in ways of seeing, new understandings of the universe, leaps of logic, and discoveries not to be imagined, even as late as last week. How much more so the serendipitous insights, the intuitive knowing, the can't-be-proved certainties that we experience when we examine our personal, private spiritual lives?

I was fascinated a number of years ago when I read a personal letter Albert Einstein wrote to a friend. Einstein told his friend about how thinking happens. He said that thinking occurs as a result of—and these are Einstein's words—"a bold leap, a speculative leap, a constructive groping." This leap, he explained, is not based on logic but on guesses and hunches.

Here is what I think is particularly useful in inquiring about things spiritual: Einstein said that this leap (a leap that happens in all genuine thinking, scientific and otherwise) is not open to inspection by others and indeed is perhaps little understood by the originators themselves. "There is," Einstein said, "no logical path to these elementary laws; only intuition, supported by being sympathetically in touch with experience."

And, the great scientist told his friend, there are two motivations that support genuine thinking: the motivation of wonder and the motivation of passion for comprehension. But, Einstein added, conditions exist. A person who does genuine thinking tolerates ambiguities and keeps unresolved problems and polarities long before the mind's eye.

As we inquire about the experiences we call spiritual, then, wonder and a passion to see clearly are approaches that will be very useful. I looked up "wonder" in the *American Heritage Dictionary* and saw that the word is associated with awe, surprise, astonishment—and puzzlement or doubt. We engage with spiritual matters in a manner that includes being available for surprises and astonishing answers, at the same time that we do not filter out our questions and doubts.

And our exploration is ignited by a passion to comprehend, a passion to make sense of our experiences. We try to be comfortable with discomfort. We pray in spite of ambiguities. At some point in this inquiry, we make Einstein's bold leap of understanding which leads us to those truths and principles by which we make decisions and choices about our spiritual lives.

We also come to accept that what we can know about our spiritual life—even with our genuine thinking—is only a small part of the whole. Einstein, again:

> *To know that what is impenetrable to us really exists, manifesting itself as the highest wisdom and the most radiant beauty, which our dull faculties can comprehend only in the most primitive forms—this knowledge, this feeling is at the center of true religiousness. . . . There is, after all, something eternal that lies beyond reach of the hand of fate and of all human delusions.*

The humility of recognizing our own "dull faculties" in light of the "highest wisdom and the most radiant beauty" is at the heart of the kind of thinking, the kind of inquiry, that is compatible with honoring our spiritual life.

## A SPIRITUAL ATTITUDE: WILLING TO GIVE ATTENTION

Having an attitude that supports the spiritual life means displaying a willingness to give attention, to be one-minded, to commit "the very nerve center of one's consent" to the source of meaning and purpose in our lives. Cultivating a spiritual attitude means we desire an ingathering of all the phases of our being into this Divine presence.

Any Scout leader who has ever shown a Girl Scout how to start a fire using a magnifying glass, any artist who has ever collected fragments of colored glass to make a mosaic, any gardener who has harvested the last crop of tomatoes, squash, and cabbage to make a thick soup, knows about ingathering.

It is a drawing together of the bits and pieces of inner and outer experiences and holding them in a center of committed attention. Such a focus is very powerful, we all know, whether in our spiritual life or in some other area, like a work project. Hermann Hesse, the German novelist, is said to have once remarked that when he started focusing on the content of his next book, even if only in his thoughts, that attention worked like a magic circle to draw in everything he would need for the book from all kinds of sources.

The same is true for our spiritual lives.

We ingather all parts of our inner and outer worlds to make sense of them in light of what we want to receive from Life—and give to Life. We are willing to pay attention to matters of the soul.

Through this focus, we draw a magic circle into which come those things that give purpose and meaning to our lives. We continue this attention-giving day after day, living our spiritual attitude.

The key word in talking about this aspect of the spiritual attitude is willingness—willingness to give attention, willingness to be one-minded. We often start with only the intention. Sometimes it takes years for that intention to transform into consistent, daily practice. For a long time after I decided to start a daily spiritual practice, that practice was likely to show up more times than not as something I hadn't done. I often felt discouraged; but then I heard someone say that everyone is always a beginner in matters of the Spirit. After that conversation, if I skipped my spiritual practice, I would just start over the next day, a beginner again, willing to give attention, to be as one-minded as I could possibly be.

Your spiritual life, then, is not defined by how totally you give attention or how one-minded you manage to be when you first begin, but by your willingness to give attention to the Divine.

Barry Lopez is a writer who inquires with openness, sees harmony, pays attention, and acknowledges the inner life. In his book *Arctic Light,* Lopez recalls walking across the frozen tundra in the Arctic and seeing tiny birds resting on the ground. He felt such a connection to Life at the moment of seeing the birds that he spontaneously folded his hands into a prayer position and made a deep bow. Recognition. Connection. Gratitude. Love. A simple spontaneous gesture of bowing to the birds. A profound demonstration of living life with a spiritual attitude.

## REFLECTION

*What parts of your life would you like to ingather?*

## SACRED TASKS

I find it valuable, from time to time, to take an inventory of the truths, beliefs, assumptions, questions, and doubts I have about the spiritual life. My friends and I do this when we gather for our bi-monthly meetings. Often, this inventory clarifies the source of a problem one of us is having in achieving her goal of daily quiet time and prayer.

For instance, one of our group not long ago realized that deep down inside what she really believed was that only saints and perhaps folks who had religious occupations could consistently keep a daily sacred quiet time. When she became aware of this assumption, she understood much more clearly why she— to use her words—gave up before she got started.

TASK: Take an inventory of the thoughts, beliefs, assumptions, questions, and doubts that make up your own "whatever am I thinking?" about the spiritual life. What decisions do you find yourself making out of this unexamined thinking?

Habits get in the way of growth and movement, especially habits of thinking. One of my old habits was wanting to know the right answer immediately. Another habit I had was wanting to be a person who always knows rather than a person who doesn't know. With thinking habits like these, if they went unchecked, how would I ever get to genuine thinking—which requires wonder, surprise, ability to live in ambiguity, a passion for seeing clearly? And, without those qualities of genuine thinking, how could I ever think with openness and possibility about the spiritual life?

TASK: What ways of thinking do you have that interfere with the kind of open, wondering mind Einstein describes? Can you identify certain habits of thinking that have a detrimental effect when you turn your mind to spiritual matters?

I can't imagine not doing my daily spiritual practice. It's my suste-
nance. It would be, for most people, like going without a cup of
coffee. I can go without my cup of coffee—even without break-
fast—but I can't go without my spiritual practice. It centers me. It
makes me aware of my true reality. It reminds me, with every
breath that I inspire, of the Spirit of God.

Over the years I have noticed that my awareness of Spirit has
continued to increase. Everything else flows from that, including
how I look at problems at work or how I handle the little things
that come up. The way I face life is shaped by my daily spiritual
discipline. There is a joy about living.

Reliance is the word that comes to me when I think about
the impact of keeping a consistent spiritual practice. I have a
reliance, as a result of my sacred time each day, that no matter what
may happen, I will be guided to handle the situation in a way that
brings joy and peace.

We live in order to learn to love; we love in order to learn to
live. No other lesson is required of us. How does a daily spiritual
practice relate to love? God is love. When we enter the silence, we
enter into timelessness, and that is where God is. Since God is love,
we discover what love is, and we are transformed!

—B. M. U., professor and holder of endowed chair,
major U. S. university

*Chapter Three*

# EXPERIENCING THE SACRED

*The interior place where we experience*
*God is the same kind of place and as real*
*as the place where we experience music*
*and poetry.*

—*Karen Armstrong*

Once, when my elderly father was ill, I stood by his hospital bed as I waited for the taxi to come to take me to the airport. My father and I both knew that this illness was probably the beginning of the last days of his life.

"We just live too far apart," my father said.

"Yes, Daddy," I replied. "Texas and Tennessee are too far apart."

A few simple words . . . but so many messages resonating in them.

As I walked down the hall to leave the hospital, my emotions and thoughts were a crazy quilt of sadness, conflict about leaving, a deep desire to have everything normal again, love, anger, a recognition that this was the inevitable, even a knowing that all was right. What was I to do with such a range of responses?

## THE EXPERIENCE OF POETRY

Then I thought of two lines of poetry that I learned many years earlier:

*I want to go home, to ride to my village gate.*
*I want to go back, but there's no road back.*

That ancient couplet, written in China in the first century, was still speaking to me in modern times. The words of the poem gathered in the feelings, thoughts, and memories that swirled around me there in the hospital. They helped make sense of my turmoil. There was the longing, the desire, the love in this moment I just had with my father. And there was the inevitability, the truth telling, the mature acknowledgment that I would need to plan my life to include this pending change that loomed enormous. Two lines of simple poetry in my head brought clarity—and even a kind of peace—to my troubled, fragmented spirit.

The French scientist Gaston Bachelard maintains that forces are manifested in poems that do not pass through the circuits of knowledge. The images in a poem, he says, don't require scholarship. They don't require understanding. The reverberations of the forces in a poem bring about a special kind of change: a change of being. When we are moved by a poem, we experience a shift that cannot be explained with one-plus-one-equals-two logic. We are different after the poem speaks to us. This is because, Bachelard reminds us, the images in a poem furnish for us one of the simplest experiences of language: language that has been lived.

Notice how immediately we can match our lives—the day we felt a renewed zest for living after a long period of lethargy and darkness, the moment we knew Life was carrying us in spite of the hard times we were going through—with the words below. We know that we have lived the language of this poem:

*For, lo, the winter is past,*
*The rain is over and gone;*

*The flowers appear on the earth;*
*The time of the singing of birds is come,*
*And the voice of the turtle is heard in the land.*

—*Song of Solomon 2:11–12*

Experiencing language that has been lived alters our being.

## THE EXPERIENCE OF MUSIC

Just as poems take us inward, music takes us away. I remember dropping in unannounced at the home of a colleague. My friend was sitting in a corner of his living room with earphones on, eyes closed, listening to an old blues album, and playing his guitar. He didn't know I was within a thousand miles, even though his preschooler was jumping around and calling my name and his wife was taking my coat. He was in a different world, having a totally different type of experience.

I think I first learned the power of music to transport the year my sister was born. In the months just before Barbara's birth, Mother needed help, so she found Annie Jones. (Annie, I thought, lived in the most wonderful place in the world—a cabin whose walls were covered top to bottom with newsprint. All those words papered everywhere—they held me spellbound for hours. I realized later that I first learned to read in Annie's cabin.)

Annie sang while she and Mother did the wash. "I Ain't Tired Yet," she belted out, twisting wet sheets. Her "Swing Low, Sweet Chariot" sounded, even to my four-year-old sensibility, like a cry for help and an unshakable hope for rescue. When she crooned, "There Is a Balm in Gilead," I felt that everything in the whole world was going to be all right: "There is a balm in Gilead to make the spirit whole. . . . "

Years later, the recordings of Mahalia Jackson helped me understand my experience as a four-year-old, listening to Annie Jones sing the old spirituals. To hear Mahalia sing "Swing Low, Sweet Chariot" is to be in touch with eons of pain, courage, and triumph that no mere prose can do justice to. When she charges forth with "Prayer Changes Things" or croons "The Love of God . . . how greater far than tongue or pen could ever tell . . . ," I hear this music in my soul, not just through my ears. Leroi Jones (now known as Amiri Baraka) is right when he says that spirituals like these summon a different quality of energy; they are unity music, uniting joy and sorrow, love and hate, hope and despair. This music is an affirmation of life, as W. E. B. Dubois observed— through all of the sorrow of the Sorrow Songs there breathes a hope, a faith in the ultimate justice of things.

Once I sat in a hall in San Francisco while a symphony played Beethoven's *Ninth*. There was a point in the evening when I suddenly "heard" geometric shapes in the music— squares, rectangles, circles. It was the strangest experience. I was hearing the music, hearing the notes, but I also was "hearing" geometric shapes. This experience continued for two or three minutes. Then there was the thought, "I am hearing truth." The closing couplet of a Keats' poem that I learned in high school flashed in my mind: "Beauty is truth, truth beauty."

What was I hearing when I "heard" geometric shapes? And how was this "hearing" truth? Perhaps my experience was related to harmonics, that phenomenon in music where one note pressed on the piano will always vibrate with higher and higher over- tones. People who are in the know on such things tell us these harmonic overtones will always be arranged in the identical order and this order is preordained by nature and ruled by universal physical law. So when I spontaneously "heard" geometrical shapes—circles, squares, rectangles—while listening that night to Beethoven's *Ninth,* perhaps I was hearing resonance of this physical law, this preordained order, this truth.

At the time, however, such information was the farthest thing from my mind. I was listening and hearing in a domain altogether different from fact and physics. Some deep part of me was awake that night in an extraordinary way. I would have to use words like: "The music carried me away. I was lost in the music, transported. The music moved me beyond words." That the experience remains so memorable today, more than a decade later, attests to its indelible and powerful marking of my interior life.

## THE IMPACT OF POETRY AND MUSIC

I remember seeing an interview on television with a person who had been injured by one of the Unabomer's deadly packages. The man told about the weeks and months following the blast. He asked his wife to play Beethoven and the works of other classical composers again and again in his hospital room. She also read Shakespeare and other poetry to him. It was the music and the poetry, he asserted, which facilitated his healing. Music and poetry reached him in a special place.

I remember falling in love when I was in high school. Something about being in that heightened state turned me into a poet and a singer (if I can use those terms loosely). I remember, even today, one poem I wrote my boyfriend after he slipped off and dated a blond beauty visiting from California:

> *The dry corn stalks cut when you walk through them*
> *But no more than you with your lying heart.*

I sang Elvis' "Love Me Tender" and Patty Page's "Tennessee Waltz" as if I were the recording artists. Falling in love had awakened some part of me I had not even known was there. I had been touched, to use the words of the quotation at the beginning of this chapter, in a real and special place.

I have a friend who is a poet and novelist—and a marvelous teacher. He explains that when we read poetry or listen to music, certain things can be explained—this composer did something like his predecessors but he did it in a new way; this poet is saying that we've lost touch with nature in a mechanized world. Other things, however, can't be known and can't be explained. This means they can't be accurately and completely represented in rational (normal) statements. The non-logical (outside of logic) things can only be experienced directly.

That is what poetry and music teach us. You have to be present to what you're experiencing. Poetry and music are only accessible on their own terms, but are also completely accessible on their own terms. That is why on one level it doesn't make any difference what poems and music pretend to be saying. It's what is happening that matters. How poetry and music change us is through an experience of what is. They expose us to the truth, what they really are.

## THE EXPERIENCE OF GOD

Thomas Merton, the writer and poet, said that we experience God in the same kind of interior place where we experience music and poetry, "only more so."

It is Merton's "only more so" that opens up wondrous possibility. Yes, we are moved in the same kind of interior place and in as real a place by music, poems, and God. But experiencing the Eternal, the Divine, *Spiritus Creator* allows something in addition to transcendence, in addition to being stirred, in addition to being taken away or taken inward. When we experience God, we experience a connection, a relationship that can serve as a source of power and direction about even the most mundane things in our daily lives. When we experience God, we experience love and the possibility of an ever increasing and expanding recognition of that love. When we experience God, we know we are not alone and we are cared for.

I remember once, while reading in the book of Isaiah, coming upon a stunning image: a city with windows of agate, foundations of sapphires, battlements of rubies, gates of sparkling jewels and borders of pleasant stones. The image was so vivid that I could see, in my mind's eye, this fantastic city, its houses, protection walls, gates and gardens. I remember getting up from my chair to go to the bookshelf to find a gem book so I could see what a carbuncle, one of the jewels mentioned in the passage, looked like. (I learned a carbuncle is a deep-red garnet, unfaceted and convex.) I even found myself painting the scene in my sketchbook. I was deeply moved, and strangely altered, by this unexpected brush with beauty. Today, fifteen years later, I still have the urge, when I think about that beautiful biblical image, to walk in gardens lined with carbuncle.

The experience of the beauty of that sacred image, however, was all the more moving because of its context: God was promising to rebuild the lives of the children of Israel who were hurt and in pain, troubled, captives of their enemies. "O thou afflicted, tossed with tempest, and not comforted, I will build you with stones of turquoise, your foundations with sapphires, and all thy borders of pleasant stones." What a promise of restoration and recreation. What a statement of compassion and care. What a symbol of love and relationship. Sometimes when I'm at my lowest, I think of this beautiful jeweled city and know it as the metaphor for which it was intended—a metaphor for the care and redemption the Divine has for all of us. For me, this is an example of the truth of Thomas Merton's "only more so."

## A FULL GAMUT OF SACRED EXPERIENCE

Sacred experience comes in many forms. It can be as quiet as a walk in a garden or as comforting as a cup of tea at the kitchen table. It can be as familiar as a favorite robe and slippers. It can also, I have learned, be funny. I never will forget the time that I burst into laughter when I came upon the singer in the Psalms who is deriding a group of enemies: "Oh, God," the singer sings, "break off their fangs. Tear out the teeth of these young lions, Lord. Let them disappear like water into thirsty ground. . . . Let them be as snails that dissolve in their own slime. . . ." (For some reason, I particularly like the "snails dissolving in their own slime" part.) I'm sure I laughed in recognition of my own outbursts when I think someone has done me wrong

It was reassuring, I must say, to take notice that even sentiments as deprecatory as this one made it into the collection of sacred songs to be sung on the way to the temple! (And Psalm 48 isn't the only angry Psalm that got included.) It is a relief to know that God welcomes an address by me, even if it is a burst of anger and resentment at somebody I don't like. I usually—and, let me quickly add, often only eventually—end up laughing at myself for being so upset and feeling relief that the gamut of spiritual experience can include this one.

All this is not to say that sacred experience is always happy experience, that when we are in touch with the Divine we know only peace, joy, promise, and resolution. We may, instead, experience what St. John of the Cross called the dark night of the soul. Our quiet time and prayer may seem like a dry, empty desert. Or, worse yet for some of us, like nothing. Just blank, void, nada. But whatever the nature of our experiences, we can say the sacred will be experienced as real, as authentic to the core of who we are, as relevant to our very Self. And, over time, we come to know these times of nothingness are only one manifestation of the full gamut of living from our spiritual center, and the full gamut includes joy, hope, and love.

## SURPRISES AND INKLINGS

Someone has called our human innate response to the Divine an *a priori* category of experience—with nothing before and with no explanation. We just have it. We don't decide to have this kind of experience. We don't plan to. Religious and spiritual experiences show up as surprises, as inklings, as intuitions, as mystery, awe, stillness, space, and energy. As moments of grace. All we can do is make ourselves available for sacred experience, put ourselves in the place to receive it, whether the experience is as still as a lazy summer afternoon or as stunning as a first view of the Rocky Mountains.

I think of a story about Flannery O'Connor, the novelist, who wrote on the dresser in the bedroom of the house she shared with her mother in Milledgeville, Georgia. When someone asked her once how she tapped into her creativity, she replied very matter-of-factly: "Every day I go in and sit at that dresser from nine o'clock to twelve. That way, if a good idea is going to come by, I'll be there to receive it."

That is the approach we can take with our attention to sacred experience. We put ourselves in a place of possibility. We commit the attention and the time. We establish a space. If a moment of grace is going to occur, we will be there to receive it. And the good news is that, perceived or not, something is always happening. During the time we spend doing our spiritual practice, something positive, powerful, and life-giving always happens.

The blues singer laments, "You gotta walk that lonesome road; you gotta take a trip down that long, long vale." The poet exults, "I made soup tonight and all my ancestors danced in the pot." We experience a sacred moment; and we quote the beautiful Psalm: "Like a deer that yearns for running streams, so my soul yearns for you, my God." We pray these words with the same exuberance as that with which the singer sings or the poet speaks.

"Only more so."

## R E F L E C T I O N

*Why do you suppose some people disparage the possibility of sacred experience when they clearly do not disparage deep and powerful responses to music and poetry?*

## SACRED TASKS

I have heard people spontaneously join in with a poet who is reciting at a poetry contest, and I have seen people cry when Willie Nelson, standing on a stage, sounds the words of "Angel Flying Too Close to the Ground." As a culture, clearly we are not embarrassed that we are deeply affected by music and poetry.

TASK: Do you remember a time when poetry and/or music became very special forms of communication for you? A time when you were carried away by the music or carried within by the poem? Did these experiences stay with you afterward? What was the difference between the experiences of music or poetry and your ordinary experiences?

Thomas Merton's statement that we experience the sacred in the same kind of interior place where we experience music and poetry, "only more so," reminds me of one of his essays where he writes about the rain.

> *The rain . . . fills the woods with an immense and confused sound. It covers the flat roof of the cabin and its porch with insistent and controlled rhythms. And I listen, because it reminds me again and again that the whole world runs by rhythms I have not yet learned to recognize . . . . What a thing it is to sit absolutely alone, in the forest, at night, cherished by this wonderful, unintelligible, perfectly innocent speech, the most comforting speech in the world, the talk that rain makes by itself all over the ridges, and the talk of the watercourses everywhere in the hollows! Nobody started it, nobody is going to stop it. It will talk as long as it wants, this rain. As long as it talks, I am going to listen.*

This must have been a moment for Thomas Merton of "only more so."

TASK: Can you recall times that you experienced, as with music or a poem, a special interior part of yourself—only more so?

There came a time in my career at NASA when I couldn't feel much satisfaction from a promotion; achievements became weaker and weaker sources of gratification. My orientation flip-flopped from doing things to make myself look good at work to experiencing a larger Life moving through me that began to refocus my priorities.

That is when my daily spiritual practice intensified. I had a practice before that point which, undoubtedly, led to the refocusing. But now my practice truly became a Way because I was letting it move through my life. This practice has allowed me to move closer to the energy, the passion of my life, to the work that is mine to do.

One of the results I see after doing this practice for several years is that new thinking occurs. I see things more clearly. I have a deeper understanding of what drives other people and what drives me. I feel more compassion and more love, more a part of the lives I touch rather than apart from them.

Meditation provides a quiet place in which to experience connection. It is a way I return to center and to stability every day. What began as discrete daily practices (and I still do the discrete daily practices) has now moved out into my entire life. I now see everything I do as an opportunity to express the awareness and centeredness that comes through my practice.

—V. W., biophysicist, author,
and business consultant

*Part Two*

*Chapter Four*

✤

# CHOOSING TO COMMIT TO A
# SPIRITUAL PRACTICE

*One does not accidentally drift toward God.*
*—Michael Casey*

In the Appalachian mountains, near where I grew up, there are still pockets of settlers tucked here and there among the coves and hollows who use verb forms that come from early Anglo-Saxon English. Instead of "She helped me," a woman might say of her neighbor who assists in making blackberry jam, "She holped me yesterday" or "She holps me every year at berry-picking time."

I think of old language usage like this when I see the word "wont," a word unusual enough to look quaint but not too strange to be useful. The dictionary says that wont means customary practice or usage. As "He is wont to say, 'I don't need help.'" Or "It's her wont to work in the garden no matter what the temperature." Our wonts identify who we are, what we are like, what we do and don't do.

## THE WONT OF SPIRITUAL PRACTICE
There is a particular wont present in the lives of people who intentionally cultivate their inner sacred life—they establish

and keep a spiritual practice. I had no idea until I was a freshman in college that anyone ever did anything related to God out of pure choice. One day during my first semester, however, I made an amazing discovery. It was the middle of the morning and I made a quick run back to my dorm room to pick up a book I had forgotten. The halls were deserted; all the girls were in class. Or at least, I thought so. But Glenna Shepherd's door was closed—in our dorm a signal usually that something was wrong.

But there was no problem.

Glenna Shepherd was having a private time of prayer. Voluntarily. For no reason except that she found it valuable to do this everyday. I was astonished. Glenna seemed like a normal girl. She was popular, involved in all kinds of school activities, scholastically tops. Yet here she was, in the middle of the morning, taking time by herself to pray.

Glenna's behavior blew to smithereens my idea that anything to do with God had to be related to obligation, threat, and fear. I had to reckon from that time forward some people choose to keep a spiritual practice for no reason except they find such a commitment personally valuable.

## A SPIRITUAL PRACTICE THAT FOCUSES ON COMMUNICATION WITH THE DIVINE

Most anything, of course, can—with the right attitude, purpose, and commitment—be a spiritual practice. Growing tomatoes and roses. Washing the dishes. Cutting wood. Doing yoga. Making cheese. Dancing. Walking. When we use such activities as the environment and the opportunity to offer gratitude, to reflect on purpose and meaning, to be quiet and mindful, we naturally are deepening our spiritual life.

But I am focusing in this book on a daily spiritual practice where stillness, quiet time, and prayer are central. Where there is an opportunity for reading and writing, music and art, reflecting, sitting in quiet, listening, asking, and meditating as specific activities. In this spiritual practice, activities are engaged in for the express purpose of putting yourself in a place to be touched by grace, taught by an inner resource, succored and sustained by the Holy Other. I'm talking about a particular type of spiritual practice that has a clear intention: That through our reflection and communication, the Divine becomes more and more the focus of our daily lives. As a result of this intentional spiritual practice, we experience more and more connection with *Spiritus Creator*. We finally, to quote the old hymn, accomplish a goal that has perhaps eluded us for years . . . to "Take Time to Be Holy."

## CREATING A MEANTIME

When we establish such a spiritual practice, we are deliberately creating a meantime in our busy lives. Like wont, the word "meantime" gets our attention because it, too, is old-fashioned enough to strike us as interesting.

We say things like, "In the meantime, I'll keep my eyes open for job opportunities you might be interested in." Or "Meantime, she invested the money, and their child's college fund grew." Or "For the meantime, let's just wait and see what happens."

Meantime is middle time. It is an intervening or intermediate period. We associate meantime with a pause, a hiatus, an interlude, a recess from strictly specified action. People who keep a spiritual practice deliberately add a period of meantime—middle time—to their lives each day. They know how necessary it is to create an interval during which they can deliberately connect with God.

## CHOOSING WHAT IS MOST IMPORTANT

A few years ago I was meeting with philosopher and writer Jacob Needleman in his home in San Francisco. We spent quite a bit of time talking about how each of us wrote our books, what we did to overcome barriers, what process worked best for us.

Near the end of the conversation, I asked Professor Needleman what he was doing at the present time, in addition to writing books. He described a seminar he had begun teaching. Very successful business people, high achieving professionals, wealthy entrepreneurs met each week to discuss the next phases of their lives. Without exception, Dr. Needleman reported, each individual in this seminar stated that she or he wanted to experience more meaning in daily life. They wanted to feel useful in ways that let them know their lives mattered. They wanted to contribute something other than money; they wanted to use their gifts and talents to make a difference in the world. Money hasn't done it, he said, reaching goals hasn't done it, being rich and famous hasn't done it. Something vital is missing that the people in this seminar are longing to add to their lives.

## A SPIRITUAL PRACTICE AND FULFILLMENT

It is during the meantime—the middle time—of a daily spiritual practice that we focus and bring to fruition desires we share with Jacob Needleman's seminar participants—to live an authentic life, to do things that really matter, to take time for what deeply fulfills us. Establishing a spiritual practice means you set aside time intentionally to honor the sacred. Stopping on a regular basis to remember who you are and what you are about gives you increasing recognition of, and access to, your gifts and talents.

Committing to this kind of daily spiritual practice makes you very proactive. This break you insert in your routine is an intentional changing of the atmosphere, an intentional setting up of an environment in which you will initiate rather than react. You are deliberate in cutting off distractions. You assert that you will, at this time, in this way, give place to the most important thing in your life, your relationship with the Divine. You will not allow something so important, something so critical to the fulfillment of who you are, to be a happenstance occurrence. In this meantime, you will carve out, by your intention, the space in which your life can take its best and most beautiful shape.

## AN ENVIRONMENT OF STILLNESS

Whatever the emphasis your spiritual practice takes on any given day, this period of meantime happens in stillness.

There is a moment of stillness that happened in my childhood which I remember today as if it just occurred. I was nine years old and visiting my grandparents on their farm in middle Georgia. It was an early summer afternoon. Grandma was at work in town, sewing doctors' coats at the cotton mill. Grandpa was taking a nap before he went back to setting out sweet potato slips. I was sitting by myself on the front porch in a tall rocking chair with big wide arms.

Maybe it was the quiet everywhere. Maybe it was the little bubbles of molecules floating in front of my eyes in the hot summer air. Maybe it was the rhythm of the rocker. But I was pulled into something I had never known, a stillness beyond all stillness. My sense heightened and I could hear the corn blades in the field next to the house scrapping in the wind. I could feel their sharp sting as much as if Grandpa and I were walking down the rows looking for roasting ears to pull for supper. I could taste the mushy fig hanging on the bush at the edge of the porch. I felt the knobby trunk of the chinaberry tree. The corn, the fig, the tree—we were all one and the same.

And I could see farther than I had ever seen—all the way across the red clay road, over the pasture, past the stile Grandma and I climbed on Wednesday nights to go to prayer meeting, into the thick woods far in the distance. I could see, in my mind's eye, back in time to the day when Daddy was a little boy and his baby brother fell into the water trough in the feed lot and drowned when nobody was looking. Back to the time the family dug to find the dishes and silverware Aunt Susanna had hidden that fateful day when Sherman's troops marched through Georgia.

It wasn't until the mailman honked to let us know Grandma's package from Sears had arrived that I returned from the stillness. Returned, but forever changed. Even as a nine-year-old, I knew something important had happened. Today I can put words to the event. In those moments I knew another reality. I experienced timelessness and transcendence. In those moments of stillness I became one with all living things.

There's a marvelous biblical story about God and stillness:

The prophet Elijah was desperately in need of help from the Divine. Elijah had just defeated King Ahab's priests in a contest to see whether Elijah's God or Baal, the god of the priests, would respond first and send fire down to consume the sacrifices. Not only had the fire from Elijah's God fallen on the altar first, but Elijah also managed to kill every priest of Baal before he left the mountain. Queen Jezebel, Ahab's wife, became furious when she heard about this defeat and swore that, before twenty-four hours had passed, Elijah would be as dead as all the Baal priests.

To escape from Jezebel's threat, Elijah went on the run for forty days and forty nights. Finally, he found a cave in which to hide on Mount Horeb. There God and Elijah had a conversation in which Elijah lamented that he was the only one of God's prophets left. "And they are trying to kill me, too," the prophet whined. God responded by telling Elijah to pay attention, that the Lord was going to pass by. The rest of the story deserves the poetry with which it is told in II Kings 19:

> *And, behold, the Lord passed by*
> *And a great and strong wind rent the mountains*
> *And brake in pieces the rocks before the Lord;*
> *But the Lord was not in the wind;*
> *And after the wind an earthquake;*
> *But the Lord was not in the earthquake;*
> *And after the earthquake a fire;*
> *But the Lord was not in the fire;*
> *And after the fire a still small voice.*
> *And it was so,*
> *When Elijah heard the still small voice*
> *That he wrapped his face in his mantle and went out.*

Mendelssohn wrote a beautiful oratorio called *Elijah,* based on this and other stories about the prophet. It is easy to imagine the wind and the fire and the earthquake in the opening sections of "Behold, God the Lord passed by!" But it is in the recitative that follows . . . Holy, holy, holy . . . that I always think of the word given to Elijah: "The Power and the Presence, God the Lord . . . these you will find only in the still, small voice . . . only in the stillness."

## RED SHOES FOREVER DANCING

You and I want stillness in our lives, but many of us feel like the little girl in the fairy tale whose red shoes would never stop dancing. The story tells us . . .

*the shoes danced the girl, rather than the other way around.
. . . so dance and dance and dance she did. Over the highest hills
and through the valleys, in the rain and the snow and in the sunlight, she danced. She danced in the darkest night and through
sunrise and she was still dancing at twilight. But it was not good
dancing. It was terrible dancing, and there was no rest for her.*

Engaging in a daily spiritual practice is one way to stop our
red shoes from dancing, a way to find the kind of stillness we feel
when we sit on a screened-in porch in a cabin in the woods listening to the rain. But very seldom in our fast-paced, loud lives
does stillness just happen. We have to create it. We have to
arrange the location, the environment, the absence of commo-
tion in which this rarity, stillness, can occur. That is the context
of a commitment to a daily spiritual practice of quiet and prayer.

In stillness we add a grace and a benediction to our lives. For a
short period, for a meantime, for a middle time, through a daily
spiritual practice, we choose to create an interval where we are in
communication with Spirit itself. In this holy stillness we find the
deep peace we most need and want in our lives. To be still with
the attention in the heart . . . all other things are beside the point.

## R E F L E C T I O N

*Can you recall a moment of stillness? What can you say about the
effect of this stillness upon you, then and now?*

### SACRED TASKS

Anytime you add something new to your daily routine, you have
to retrain your environment. A friend who wanted to start a quiet

time in her life told me: "One thing that will interfere with my establishing a daily spiritual discipline is the habit I have of turning on the television the minute I wake up." I asked her what would help her make the change; and she answered, "My deep desire to have more peace and balance in my daily life."

TASK: Make a list of your wonts: The ones that will work for, the ones that will work against, your establishing a daily spiritual discipline.

There are established meantimes in life: the Sabbath, sabbaticals, sick days, personal days, and vacations. Many of these intervals are so ingrained in the culture there is outside support for including them in our lives. The meantime for a daily spiritual discipline, however, usually has no outside support. It will occur only because you want and create it.

TASK: Ask: What kinds of meantimes are already present in my life? What is attractive about adding a new one that I dedicate to my sacred Self? Think about what you need to do to maintain a spiritual meantime, a middle time, in your life.

When I don't do my spiritual discipline, I lose the richness of my life. I am carried away into mundane, trivial things. Knowing God's purpose for my life is the most important thing to me, and I need daily quiet time so that I can listen. My spiritual practice, too, is a safe place, a place where I am nourished and protected. I then take these qualities out into my day.

As an artist, my daily spiritual practice is a way of letting go of things that clog up my creativity. I get rid of things that are frustrating and irritating. The boulders are removed from the river and the river can flow. I can be surprised by ideas, thoughts, and images that come spontaneously.

If I have a guitar in my hand, the surprise may be new melodies and lyrics. If I have a pen in my hand, the surprise can be ideas that pop into my head. If I have a brush in my hand, the painting is fresh, not labored. It has soul. Without my daily spiritual practice, my work soon becomes heavy, labored, and full of conflict. I have failed to realize the potential of many a painting and a song by being muddied in my mind and spirit . . . and my quiet time each day helps keep that mud washed out.

—C. O., painter and songwriter

Chapter Five

🪁

# CREATING THE SPACE AND MAKING THE TIME

*I have a great deal of company in the house, especially in the morning when nobody calls.*

—Henry David Thoreau

I remember when my mother, well past retirement age, decided to start an exercise program. I came home to Possum Creek, Tennessee, one spring. Leaning up against the front door was a long oak stick, clean of bark and snags and tapered at the end. "My walking companion," Mother said. "Your daddy whittled it for me."

"What inspired you to start walking?" I asked. "I heard that Minnie had stopped smoking at age ninety-four—before it harmed her health, she said—so I decided I'd start exercising to keep my good health," my mother answered.

I took notice of how my mother structured her exercise program. After that critical first step—her decision to start walking—she took the next action. Because she lived in the mountains, near only narrow two-lane roads, she had to trace out a walking route that was as free from hazard as possible. "I've got a one-mile circuit that goes up to the gate and down by the creek," she explained. She put into place a plan. "I keep a record on the calendar of every day I walk and how long it takes me." Over the years Mother's practice of daily exercise evolved. For her birthday one year, my husband and I gave her a membership in the *Prevention* magazine walking club. The organization provided her with an official record book in which to chart her activities. When she sent the information in from time to time, honor patches for hours walked arrived back in the mail. She got a stop watch so she would have an accurate measure of the time. My sister and I took her to the walking club's annual convention in San Diego. She won a beautiful wooden plaque for completing five hundred hours of walking. She read and got smarter about getting the most out of her exercise—"You've got to swing your arms more, Sister," she instructed when I joined her. Some years she walked more; some less. But over time she became a permanent, always-learning, always-growing walker. (One of the last things my sister and I took from the dining room wall of our parents' home after their deaths was Mother's ribbon covered with all her walking club patches and that treasured wooden plaque.)

## MAKING THE DECISION

My mother's actions can be applied, I think, to initiating your spiritual practice. First comes the internal decision: I will establish a daily quiet time. Nothing will happen without that internal decision. And that internal decision will be based on something that has meaning: innate desire, feeling nudged inwardly, reading, listening to someone talk about the subject, the example of some-one admired. It may be months—even years—in coming, this internal decision to add a dedicated time for spiritual growth and development.

## MAKING THE TIME

Following the internal decision, you must have a structure. You need a time and a place. Let's deal with time first.

None of us has enough time. We don't have enough time to exercise. We don't have enough time to do the housework. We don't have enough time to see friends. We all feel buffeted, pushed, and pulled with this demand, that desire, this necessity. That is certainly one legitimate way to think about and experience time.

But then there are other ways to think about time. Not until the year 1345 was the hour divided into minutes and seconds. Not until the 1500s was it thought necessary to add a minute hand to clocks. Before these hours and minutes allowed people to "keep time," folks lived a daily round of time: sunrise, day, sunset, and night.

So even though you and I live today with clocks that can measure nanoseconds, we also live, during each twenty-four hours, one daily round that contains all the time there is in the world. The next day we live a round that contains all the time there is in the world. Every sunrise, noon, sunset, and night you and I have all the time in the world. Every twenty-four hours we have all the time there is in the world.

## ALL THE TIME IN THE WORLD

When I think about how I'm often tempted to rumble on about not having enough time, I laugh. None of my friends nor I ever say something like, "There isn't enough surface on this planet." Now, we might say something about the dangers of overpopulation, something about our concerns for the health of the planet, something about the fragile balance on the planet, but we never say, "Oh, me, this planet isn't big enough. There isn't enough surface on the planet." Somehow—unlike the round of time each day—we accept the size of the planet. We don't lament its circumference. We don't complain that the planet is too small. We would probably feel ridiculous if we did.

Yet, I find myself doing this with time and never even cracking a smile. "There just isn't enough time," I will say, full of tension and regret. When, really, I have, every twenty-four hour period, all the time in the world. Saying, "I don't have time to do this; I don't have time to do that," then, points toward something other than the actual number of hours in the day.

When we look at someone whose life is not dictated by the pressure of time (and most of us probably have met at least one of these rare people), the person who never seems rushed or frantic about the clock, what we see is someone who does realize she has all the time there is in the world, twenty-four hours every day. We see someone who knows that the answer to any stress and strain about time rests in his decisions about how that time will be used. What priorities will be kept? What extras culled out? What adult decisions will be made about possible ways to use all the time in the world we are given every day?

A friend recently showed me a box of Tazo Wild Sweet Orange Tea. On the back was a list of the ingredients in the tea and an address to send for a catalog. Following the catalog address appeared these words: "Allow two weeks of this lifetime for a response." My friend and I opined that the copy writer for this tea company understands the concept "all the time in the world" and understands all the decisions we make exist inside this total amount of time that will never be stretched or shortened.

## GREAT TO BE BUSY

Another novel way to think about time is to consider that it is great to be busy. I enjoy reading the ancient wisdom literature. The writer of Ecclesiastes, someone with a sharp tongue and a great sense of humor, instructs: "Work hard at whatever you do, because there will be no actions, no thought, no knowledge, no wisdom in the world of the dead—and that is where we are all going."

Well, that's blunt, isn't it? Being busy, in this line of thought, is a plus for the living because you can't be busy when you are dead.

It was the same wisdom teacher who said:

*It is good and fitting for one to eat and drink and to enjoy the good of all her labor in which she toils under the sun all the days of her life which God gives her, for it is her heritage. As for every woman to whom God has given riches and wealth and given her power to eat of it, to receive her heritage and rejoice in her labor, this is the gift of God. For she will not dwell unduly on the days of her life because God keeps her busy with the joys of her heart.*

We can think, then: "It is great to be busy—provided what I am busy with is the joys of my heart." We have the same type of opportunity to ask—"Is what I am busy with the joys of my heart?"—as we have to think—"I have every day all the time there is in the world." We then make the choices for how we will spend that twenty-four hour round.

I remember talking to a friend who said she was astonished one day to realize how many things she was doing out of habit or others' expectations that she really didn't like doing: going to a study group that had outlived its interest for her, playing golf because her friends needed her to make a foursome, doing the same volunteer work she had done for fifteen years because the situation and people were familiar. "What I really want to do now," she said, "is to study genealogy, learn to play tennis, and give some time to tutoring children in reading." She was taking stock of how she spent her twenty-four hours each day and deciding to make some new choices.

## FLEXIBLE TIME

There is another piece of good news related to time and establishing a daily spiritual practice. The amount of time we spend is whatever we decide to spend. There are no rules, no minimum and maximum, no "You have to take this amount of time." The way I figure it is this: If Jesus could take five loaves and two fishes and bless them; and then five thousand men plus all the women and the children have enough to eat, with twelve baskets full of leftovers at the end of lunch . . . then whatever amount of time I can give to my daily spiritual practice will be blessed and I will experience outcomes exponentially.

A woman I know has three young children, two of whom are pre-schoolers. I knew she kept a spiritual discipline so one day I asked: "How in the world do you do it? How do you create the time?" She answered: "One thing I've learned to do is to start the quiet time with the children present, although they don't know that is what I am doing. For instance, if I am rocking the baby to sleep, I sit there as long as I can with her so that I can have my quiet time and prayer while she is sleeping. I will also draw and color with the two older children. While they are making their pictures, I am making mine, which might be my best attempt at capturing my internal state on that particular day.

She explained that she often had to divide the parts of her spiritual discipline, doing one part at one time and another later. Either after the kids have gone to bed or before they get up in the morning, she takes some time for sitting in silence. There are periods, however, when the best she can manage, she said, is a lot of mini-quiet times throughout the day or in the middle of the night. "These are moments when I pause, stand or sit still, and think about God. My spoken prayers often occur at bedtime when I pray aloud with the children."

So, the answer? Whatever amount of time I choose. I have all the time there is in the world—I have the full twenty-four hour span that is all the time there is in the world anywhere on this globe. And it is OK to be busy. I am happy to be busy because that means I am alive and not dead. I am busy because I can choose to do things related to the joys of my heart.

All I need to start a process of developing my spiritual life is some dedicated time. Time set aside specifically for the sacred. Fifteen minutes is an excellent place to start. But so is sixty seconds or three minutes (one of my friends even uses an egg timer!) or an hour, if that is the amount of dedicated time you choose to give. I've known more than one person whose commitment began at less than five minutes who will tell you today that he or she has a deep, growing, satisfying spiritual life and a consistent daily spiritual practice. The point is: some amount of dedicated time.

## CREATING A SACRED SPACE

Boundaries mark the end of one kind of activity and the beginning of another. If this boundary has some physical component to it instead of existing only in our minds, the finishing of one activity and the start of another activity is more sharp and vivid. I notice I am aware I have finished doing the dinner dishes when I wipe off all the counters and then spread the dishcloth on the sink to dry. I wipe my hands on a nearby tea towel and turn to do something else. The spread wet dishcloth and the dry tea towel mark the physical boundary of a specific activity—washing the dinner dishes.

In a wonderful trilogy of books about designing and building, architect Christopher Alexander talks about the boundaries of sacred spaces. Traditional societies, he says, have always recognized the importance of sacred sites. Mountains are marked as places of pilgrimage; rivers become holy; a building, a tree, or a stone takes on power through which people can connect to the Divine.

One of the patterns of architectural language that Alexander identifies as central to a place we associate with the sacred is some kind of physical boundary. Something about the physical shape of the location, or the way the space is organized, or the contents of the place we choose for our daily spiritual practice needs to serve as a boundary, a symbolic gateway, between the other parts of our lives and this.

## A PHYSICAL GATEWAY

How might we create such a bounded space—a symbolic gateway—in which to engage in our daily spiritual practice?

The physical space itself in which we carry out our spiritual discipline represents a gateway. This gateway might be a corner of a room set aside for a daily spiritual practice, the corner perhaps demarcated by a screen, a rug or a collection of sacred symbols. Or the physical space might be one specific chair in a room that is used by others in the family and for many purposes. Once, early in our marriage, my husband and I were invited to dinner at the home of our landlords. During a tour of the house prior to eating, Mrs. Patra, a successful ceramist and businesswoman, pointed to a rocker in the bedroom she and her husband shared and said in a soft voice, "That is where I meditate and pray every morning." Her quiet declaration made an enormous impact on me.

In our home, my husband and I have two symbolic gateways that mark the physical space dedicated to the sacred. In our bedroom we have a low, two-shelf white bookcase that serves as an altar. On this altar we have probably half a dozen votive candles in crystal holders and various religious objects that have meaning for us. On either side of the altar, we have our easy chairs—mine a chaise lounge and his a big, overstuffed armchair. When we are ready for our quiet time and prayer in the morning—something we try to do together every day—we light the candles and then sit in our chairs. This space and these actions mark a boundary for us and an entrance into the holy. The second physical space is in our guest bedroom. To one side, in a kind of alcove, there is a chair, a small bench that holds candles and books, and space to do whatever activity is associated with quiet time. This is my other sacred space in the house . . . where I write in my journal, do collages, listen to music, look out at the trees in our backyard, whatever I am doing that day to come to quiet. It is also where I sit in silence and pray.

The idea of building or creating a space that is only used for meditation, quiet, and prayer has, in the past few years, become mainstream. People are including atriums, garden rooms, chapels, prayer and meditation spaces in their homes as separate sacred locations. One person I know who lives in a busy city plans to build a poustinia—a small one-room building for reflection and prayer—at the far edge of her backyard. Clearly, there are many ways to think about creating sacred space.

## A ROVING SPACE

It may be for many of us that the location where we carry out our daily spiritual practice is a roving one. Perhaps the kitchen table close to the stove one wintry morning; perhaps the glider in the yard on a beautiful spring day; perhaps a sofa in the den at night after everyone has gone to sleep. When the physical location, because it changes, cannot mark the gateway between what we were doing before and the dedicated time for our spiritual practice, we can provide that boundary by what we bring with us into the space.

One of my friends, the mother of young children, marks her spiritual practice spot with a little white wire basket. In this basket she keeps the reading material for her spiritual practice, a journal book, a small tape recorder, a small sketch pad, and a box of crayons—which more times than not turns out to be missing, only to be located in the kids' toy box. "Wherever I take my wire basket is my spiritual practice place for that day," she reports.

Another friend travels a lot in her work. Quiet time and prayer are a given for her each day, so she has a small zippered pouch in which she carries what she needs: her reading material, journal, a candle (the kind that comes in a tin can), and music tapes. This pouch comes out, she says, with her cosmetics, goes on the table by the bed, and is ready for her quiet time and prayer each morning.

A man I know whose job also involves traveling—he leaves home every Sunday afternoon and returns on Friday—manages, even in his temporary hotel quarters, to have what he refers to as his prayer and devotion time each day. He uses a Bible, perhaps a spiritual book—recently, one by Catherine Marshall on gratitude—and writing material.

Sacred spaces for quiet time and prayer are as varied as the people who use them and the circumstances in which they find themselves, whether at home or on the road. Some people I know have a small altar, pillows on the floor, and an incense burner nearby. Some like a totally undecorated space—nothing but walls, floor, perhaps a prayer rug or a pillow to sit on. For one man I know, his sacred space is a recliner with a Bible and a pencil and pad nearby. One friend uses her home office because she does her spiritual discipline before business hours. One has a small prayer rail with a padded cushion made from an altar that had been replaced when her church was remodeled. Another sits at the kitchen table with a cup of hot tea, looking out on the patio where she grows flowers year-round. A friend who lives in a big city told me she uses the same corner of the couch every day because she lives in a small apartment. "Sacred space is now open," she said to me, laughing. "That's what I say," she elaborated, "when I pick up whatever I'm going to use that day in my sacred quiet time and sit down on that particular end of the sofa."

The important thing is that something—the physical space itself, the items we bring to the location, the ritual of the activities we engage in—signal a gateway for us, a passage from the activities before to the experience of engaging on this yet another day or evening in our dedicated spiritual practice.

## GATEWAY AS INVITATION

I noticed an obituary recently in the *New York Times*. The woman who died at age eighty-seven, Emily Whaley of Charleston, South Carolina, was described like this:

> *. . . with a green thumb and such an eye for color . . . she helped show flowering Charleston there was bloom beyond azaleas and camellias and turned her backyard into one of the nation's most acclaimed private gardens. . . . one of the first gardeners to dare to plant for year-round blooms . . . Mrs. Whaley helped establish a trend of planting perennials like roses, gerbera daisies and hydrangeas, in front of the towering azalea and camellia shrubs.*

This paragraph of the obituary especially caught my eye:

> *A woman so attuned to the subtleties of nature that she was forever commenting on the weather and could become ecstatic over*

*the feel of a gentle breeze on the back of her neck, Mrs. Whaley*
*. . . was comfortable speaking in epigrams. A secluded garden*
*bench, for example, was "a place to invite your soul for a visit."*

I wish I had been privileged to know Emily Whaley. According to the obituary, not only did she garden but she also was an accomplished pianist and ballroom dancer and once taught chess. She also, the *Times* reported, "had a way with the stove." A book of her family recipes and stories will be published posthumously. I suspect she found many, many ways to create the time and space to "invite her soul for a visit."

Creating the space and making the time . . . that is our opportunity when we decide to include in our days a spiritual practice. We are establishing a place and giving the minutes that make it possible for us to fulfill a deep need and desire. By creating a sacred space and stepping out of our busy lives for a few minutes every day, we find quiet and stillness. In this we, too, have an opportunity to invite our souls for a visit.

## R E F L E C T I O N

*Do you remember a time when you invited your soul for a visit?*

### SACRED TASKS

One way I started thinking about the twenty-four-hour cycle of a day is comparing it to my closet. I have only so much room in my closet so it has become a customary practice for me, from time to time, to cull what I no longer need. Similarly, I have the twenty-four hours a day to spend however I decide, based on my commitments, desires, and values. I ask myself what clutter takes up time during which I could be doing something I'd rather do? What could I stop doing?

TASK: Take an inventory of how you spend your time. Are there some things that fill your twenty-four hours each day that are no longer satisfying or useful to you? Are there other things you would rather be doing? What, among your activities, could you eliminate or change so you have more time for the things that draw you or interest you now?

You can find inspiring books on creating sacred spaces in your home and its surroundings. Suggestions range from setting aside a whole room or area to looking at ordinary parts of the house—windows, doors, floors, and ceiling—as patterns and forms that can remind you of the spiritual. "Finding the Sacred in Everyday Architecture" is the subtitle of a book I recently bought called *The Temple in the House.* Another recent purchase, *Cultivating Sacred Space: Gardening for the Soul,* is a book as beautiful as it is inspiring.

TASK: Consider how you would create a sacred space in your home and its surroundings. Would the space be stationary or roving? What materials, objects, and resources would you want close by? What about this space would make it seem like a gateway to the holy?

At age eight, I saw a picture in *Life* magazine: three ethereal figures, heads bowed, proceeded down the aisle of a cathedral from the Middle Ages. Their flowing capes and wide monks' hoods spoke of a world so other than the one I lived in . . . yet I recognized that world. The peculiar thing about the picture was that the figures looked truncated, as if they were walking on their knees. The article—on the subject of apparitions and departed spirits—explained: The photo was taken in the church as it stands today. The monks died centuries ago, before the floor had been raised two feet. In the picture, the ghostly figures are walking on the original floor, the floor beneath the floor.

I've always known it was there . . . the floor beneath the floor, that reality from which all is and arises. Sometimes I would even drop down to it, usually quite by accident. I walked mainly on the false floor.

I had no real intention of starting a daily spiritual practice. It was some below-consciousness knowing that roused me to go sit, focus on my breath, and repeat, silently, the only plea I could think of: "Dear One, Dear One, Dear One." I didn't ask or hope for anything. But I kept getting up every morning and sitting. And something began to change. I began not to understand but to experience the meaning of "be in the world, but not of it." I was settling into the ground of another world. I now live in that reality, not every day, but many days. And every day I make myself present for it, by sitting in stillness, lighting a candle, quieting all thought.

Don't think I'm bragging about my discipline. If I could have found an easier way to do this—or, better yet, to get out of doing it—believe me, I would have. There is none.

—L. H., licensed professional
counselor and writer

# Chapter Six

# DESCRIBING A SPIRITUAL PRACTICE

*Every good story has a beginning, a middle, and an end.*

—*Anonymous*

$\mathbf{M}$y great-grandparents John and Susan Harper emigrated from Ireland in the mid 1800s and settled as farmers in Georgia, about forty miles south of Atlanta. While the Harpers tried not to advertise their heritage—being Irish was not something good to be in Georgia in those years, my father told me once—everything from the name Harper to Grandpa John's red hair and fiery temper marked them as Eire's own.

Some of the most Irish gifts of my heritage I learned from my father. The land was so important to him and his family that every area of the Harper homeplace had a name: The Shallows, the South Boundary, the North Pasture, the Dip. He could still recite those names when he was almost ninety. In fact, near the end of his life, he drew me a map, after dreaming the night before about the land. On the map was every section of the acreage which he and his family farmed, each section marked with its individual name.

And the cycles of the year, particularly the phases of the moon and their effect on planting—these were very important.

Even though our father had a career as a minister, he grew things his entire life—tomatoes in buckets, blackberries on vines that stretched across wire at the side of the yard, sweet potatoes, all kinds of greens. (The last letter he wrote before he died was to *The Georgia Farm and Consumer Bulletin,* asking for information on how to grow sweet potatoes in a tin tub like the ones the publication had shown recently in a photograph.) He always checked the *Farmer's Almanac* to find out the right time to plant this crop or that, and that right time depended on the phases of the moon.

## CELTIC WAY OF PRAYING

A few years ago a lot began to be written about Celtic spirituality and the Celtic way of praying. Because of my Irish heritage of attachment to the land and alignment with the cycles of nature, I felt immediately at home with the emphasis of these prayers.

Listen to this ancient Irish prayer about the land:

*Facing the south for warmth*
*A little stream across its ground*
*A choice plot with abundant bounties*
*Which would be good for every plant. . . .*

And this one, about the right day for planting:

*I will go out to sow the seed,*
*In name of God who gave it growth . . .*
*Friday, day auspicious*
*The dew will come down to welcome*
*Every seed that lay in sleep*
*Since the coming of cold without mercy;*

*Every seed will take root in the earth,*
*As the King of the elements desired. . . .*

Nothing considered too trivial to be the subject of prayer. All can be holy. All can be blessed.

## THE NUMBER THREE

One thing I noticed soon after beginning to read Irish prayers is the appearance again and again of the number three. Three folds of the cloth . . . three leaves of the shamrock . . . the three persons of the Trinity. In the *Carmina Gadelica,* a collection of poems, songs, prayers, and blessings handed down from generation to generation in Ireland, Scotland, and Wales, there is a description of a daily way of praying based on the number three.

> *The embers were spread evenly on the hearth in the middle of the floor and formed into a circle with a small boss, or raised heap, left in the middle. This circle was then divided into three equal sections with a peat laid between each section, each peat touching the boss, which was called the Hearth of the Three which formed the common center. The first peat was laid down in the name of the God of Life, the second in the God of Peace, and the third in the God of Grace. The circle would then be covered over with ashes sufficient to subdue, but not extinguish, the flame in the name of the Three of Light.*

## THREE PARTS OF A SPIRITUAL PRACTICE

One day when I was thinking about the repetition of threes in the Celtic way of praying I realized the similarity with another set of three. For hundreds of years people have written and spoken about the three parts of a daily spiritual practice. There is, first, some kind of activity that announces, that demarcates this activity from what came before and represents coming to stillness. Perhaps this initial action of the spiritual practice is the reading of a sacred Scripture or other inspirational piece. Perhaps it is writing in a journal, listening to a song, drawing a picture. Perhaps it's a bell or a gong sounding, or a candle being lit. Perhaps it is the invocation of the Sacred in some personal way.

Second, there is the period of stillness.

Third, some kind of ending: Intercessory prayer, thanksgiving, the gathering of thoughts for application to the day ahead, some way of acknowledging the completion of this time that has been devoted to centering one's being in the Eternal.

## A LIGHT-HEARTED AND PRACTICAL EXAMPLE

One of the most interesting accounts of someone teaching the three parts of a daily spiritual practice is the delightful instructions which Francis de Sales, a beloved cleric and teacher living in France in the seventeenth century, provided to his young kinswoman, Marie de Charmoisy. What started out to be only notes for Mme. Charmoisy turned into a book that was published in 1607. (This book, *Introduction to the Devout Life,* became so popular it was translated into seventeen languages in a short span of time and remains a favored classic today.)

One of the many things I like about his instructions is that long before the modern emphasis on "the whole person," Francis included all parts of our human makeup when he taught how to carry out a daily spiritual discipline. He emphasized the imagination: we might start by picturing in our minds the ways the

Divine shows up in our lives, for example. He uses the intellect: next, choose a question about the meaning of your life and ponder on that question in stillness. He adds the emotional (think of the needs of someone else) and the physical (take something from this time of reflection and prayer back out into real life and apply it there during the rounds of your day) and the communal (pray for others and for yourself).

Francis agreed to publish the instructions so not only Marie but all persons who wished to do so, could change their desire for a daily spiritual practice into a solid resolution. A daily spiritual practice, Francis insisted, was as open to soldiers, domestics, shopkeepers, courtiers, statesmen, people of affairs, and individuals in their homes as it was to solitaries in the desert and nuns in their cells. (Francis was especially committed to the education of women at a time in history when such a commitment was an anomaly. He and his colleague Jane de Chantal opened at least thirteen schools for girls and women.)

Another thing I like about Francis' instructions—which illustrate the principle of three parts of a spiritual discipline—is their good sense, the balance, and their down-to-earth style. He thinks, for instance, that having money is a fine thing: "So also you can possess riches without being poisoned by them if you merely keep them in your home and purse and not in your heart." Francis encourages people to enjoy what they wear: "For my part, I would have devout people, whether men or women, always the best dressed in a group but the least pompous and affected." Francis likes to use images that appeal to the senses: "bouquets from a garden, the refreshing smell of cinnamon, bees making honey, ships, horses, birds, tailors, saffron and topaz, plants that grow green and flourish." None of the stern, stark ascetic approach to the spiritual life for him.

## USE YOUR IMAGINATION TO PLACE YOURSELF IN THE PRESENCE OF GOD

Marie, for whom Francis wrote the spiritual discipline instructions, had been a maid of honor in the household of Catherine of Cleves. In 1600 she married Francis' relative, Claude de Charmoisy. A few years later, Marie and Claude, who was ambassador of the Duke of Savoy, were involved in a lawsuit, probably something to do with the ownership of land. This lawsuit kept the couple living near Francis for the entire winter. During this time, Marie made her request for instructions. That request resulted in Francis writing out the procedures of the three parts of a daily spiritual practice: "I will give you a short, simple method. First . . . the preparatory part. Place yourself in the presence of God. . . . Remember God is present in a most particular manner in your heart and in the very center of your spirit."

Here Francis suggests some principal means that Marie might use to place herself in the holy Presence. Each method focuses on the use of the imagination. She might, for example, picture the absolute presence of the Divine, that is, picture God being present in all things and in all places. . . . "Just as wherever birds fly they always encounter the air, so also wherever we go or wherever we are we find God present."

She also might picture in her mind the ways the Divine shows up in her specific life. "God is present," he says, "in a most particular manner in her heart and in the very center of her spirit, animating and enlivening her in ways specific to who she is." She might imagine herself being looked at by the Divine. "This is by no means a mere figment of the imagination but the very truth. Although we do not see the Divine, it remains true that from on high the Divine beholds us." I personally like this particular imaginative entry to the presence of the holy. There is a verse in Isaiah that I often use to come to quiet. In this verse the voice of the Lord is heard to say,

*I will quietly look from my dwelling*
*Like clear heat in sunshine*
*Like a cloud of dew in the heat of harvest.*

I imagine myself in the midst of that beam of sunshine, refreshed by the cloud of dew.

Marie might also imagine herself in a scene with the Divine. "Just as we sometimes imagine a friend to be present and say, I imagine that I see such a one who is doing this or that ... " she can imagine herself in a setting or situation with the Holy Other. Practical to the last degree, Francis ends the instructions by saying: "Do not use them all at once, but only one at a time and that briefly and simply."

## USE YOUR MIND TO CONSIDER SOME MEANINGFUL THOUGHT

Francis then describes the second part of the spiritual practice. Marie should next meditate on some spiritual thought that has enough "appeal, light, and fruit" to keep her interest.

*After the imagination has done its part there follows the act of the intellect and this we term meditation. Imitate the bees, who do not leave a flower as long as they can extract any honey out of it. But if you do not come on anything that appeals to you after you have examined and tried it for a while, then go on to another, but proceed calmly and simply in this manner and do not rush yourself.*

One thing she might meditate on, he suggests, is holy prayers she had learned, perhaps as a child. She can also inquire and meditate on the answer to a question like: "Consider that a

certain number of years ago you were not yet in the world . . .
My soul, where were we at that time?" She might ponder:
"Consider the nature God has given to you. It is the highest in
this visible world; it is capable of eternal life and of being per-
fectly united to Divine Majesty." She might return thanks: "My
great and good Creator, how great is my debt to you . . . " Whatever she chooses as the subject of her meditation, Marie is to
carry out this meditation in quietness and stillness. "Do not
hurry along and say many things . . . "

## TAKE ACTION, GIVE THANKS, AND PRAY FOR OTHERS

The third part of the daily spiritual practice Francis teaches to
Marie is the conclusion. She should, after finishing her meditation, make some sort of special resolution to focus on for this
day ahead . . . for example, "I won't be offended by this person
or that." This allows her to apply her daily spiritual practice
directly to the rest of the day's activities. Then she is to give
thanks and, finally, complete her daily spiritual practice by praying her vocal prayers: prayers for her own needs, the needs of
others, and the needs of the world.

This third step in Marie's daily spiritual practice allows her,
Francis says, to "gather a little devotional bouquet."

*I explain my meaning. People who have been walking about
in a beautiful garden do not like to leave without gathering in
their hands four or five flowers to smell and keep for the rest of
the day. In the same way, when our soul has carefully considered by meditation a certain mystery we should select one, two,
or three points that we liked best and that are most adapted to
our improvement on which to think frequently.*

## MODERN-DAY EXAMPLES

Someone talking today might describe her adaptation of Francis' three-part daily spiritual practice like this:

- a cup of coffee and the *New York Times,* followed by some piece of inspirational reading that lifts my thinking
- a period of time spent sitting on the patio, eyes closed, ears open to the sounds around me and to the words whispered in my own heart
- prayers of request, followed by prayers of gratitude.

There is, of course, no right way to do the three parts of a daily spiritual practice. Inside an over-all structure, people do a multitude of things and take a multitude of approaches. Listen to the variety in these individuals' accounts of their practice:

One person says:

*I begin by saying something simple like the verse from Psalms, "Be still and know that I am God." Then I choose a word for my mind to focus on . . . a word like "love" or "silence" or a prayer like "Make me an instrument of Thy Peace." I focus my mind on this word or prayer for a few minutes. Then when I've finished, I ask for help and guidance for the day and I pray specifically for my family.*

Another person recounts:

*If something is bothering me when it's time for my daily spiritual practice, I will say to myself, "I've got to do something to bring all the pieces of myself here." I often write in my journal. One of the things I frequently write is a letter to God. There's a story in the Old Testament that inspires me: King Hezekiah is at his wit's end because an enemy king is about to decimate Hezekiah's kingdom. With nothing left to do, Hezekiah takes the threatening letter from his enemy and spreads it out on the altar in the temple. He tells God that only divine intervention can save them from the devastation promised in this letter. When in dire need, I take a cue from Hezekiah, write a letter outlining all that is wrong, and metaphorically spread it on the altar.*

*After this I might read something or I might move right into my sit-and-listen activity. Here I often repeat a prayer or the Twenty-third Psalm in my head. This concentrates my mind and makes it possible for me to listen to my heart. This still, quiet period is the most important part of the practice for me. During this time I have remembered valuable things I hadn't thought of in years or I have become calm and centered after being agitated for days or I have experienced a rush of love that goes far beyond the people and things in my immediate environment. When I finish the still time of being quiet and listening, it's time for me to talk. That's when I pray.*

A third person describes the spiritual discipline time like this:

*In my special room, at my library table, I first carry out several rituals that have meaning for me. Then I light a candle and settle myself in a chair.*

*In my chair I wrap myself in a throw which has the moon and stars woven into the fabric. Thomas Moore, the writer, says every home should contain a symbol of the heavens. This is mine.*

*I read a few pages or a chapter from a spiritual book. (I'm currently using John Main's* The Way of Unknowing.*) These books tend to focus on the message that our goal is to find the Kingdom at hand or to be released from the wheel of samsara (suffering), to leave self (ego) behind.*

*I meditate for thirty minutes, repeating the word Maranatha (Aramaic for "Lord, come") with eyes closed. At the end of my*

*meditation I say Amen and do a few closing rituals. These
include praying that I may have an open ear, open mind, open
hands, open eyes—and the courage to follow where You would
lead me. Then I conclude by blowing out the candle on the table.*

## THREE PARTS CREATING A WHOLE

There is nothing magic, of course, about the three parts of a daily
spiritual practice. There is no rule that you have to do it this way.
Each segment or part does, however, serve a different purpose.

The opening activity for spiritual practice is designed to
bracket what came before from this specific sacred time that you
are now beginning. What you do first allows you to ingather the
bits and pieces of your life. To name this period. To distinguish
between the part of yourself that—remembering Emerson's wonderful words—has aunts and uncles and must go buy turnips and
apples from the part of yourself that is interior, timeless, wise, and
deep. Whether your opening activity includes music, art, dance,
writing, lighting candles, listing things for which you are grateful,
or reading something inspiring, do something that begins to connect you with yourself. Something that quiets, deepens, calms.
Something that brings you to stillness.

The middle activity—sitting in silence—many assert is the
most fruitful of all the things you can do in your spiritual practice. Here you listen. You provide an opportunity for your spirit
to experience its connection to the all-powerful *Spiritus Creator.*
Kierkegaard once said, "A man prayed and first he thought that
prayer was talking, but he became more and more quiet until in
the end he realized that prayer was listening." This middle part
of your daily spiritual practice is a listening prayer.

John Lewis, the civil rights leader and United States Con-
gressman from Georgia, calls this a period of silence "simply

having an executive session with yourself. It's a period of being alone, a period of meditation, a period of quiet and just being you." Richard Foster, a masterful writer on prayer, as well as other spiritual disciplines, describes this middle period in his daily practice this way:

> *Meditation is one of the most basic forms of listening prayer. Usually it's tied to a passage of Scripture. Other times it can move more deeply into what is usually thought of as contemplation, in which, as French author J. N. Grou prayed, "Oh, Divine Master, teach me this mute language that says so much." So there is silence, listening prayer, and meditation. These must be a regular part of our prayer experience because it isn't just a matter of us talking. . . .*

He goes on to describe the value of this middle part, this listening in silence:

> *I often gain focus . . . and out of that I seek to live my day. I find I am more on target and have a greater sense of confidence and strength in which I am doing, so that I am living the day out of the guidance that [this kind of silent] prayer gives me.*

The last activity—praying for ourselves and for others—connects us with the world around us and with our commitment to contribute to that world. Prayer takes our love out. It causes things to happen. It makes us a part of a network. It allows us to use the power that came from the inner stillness to do good in the world. It is what allows us to act in the world, to be a person of wisdom, balance, and wholeness more often than we would be if we didn't pray.

So goes the three-part daily spiritual practice, with all carrying out the three activities in their personal way, but all experiencing the benefits and value of each segment of the spiritual practice. Hasidic Jewish writings often compare the soul to a flame, burning with a constant love of God, seeking at every moment to rise upward to its source. "The soul . . . is a candle of God, searching out all the chambers of the heart." The three parts of your daily spiritual discipline provide a concrete, practical means for this searching into all the chambers of your heart.

## R E F L E C T I O N

*Does Francis de Sales' approach to spiritual practice suggest any possibilities for your sacred quiet time?*

## SACRED TASK

In my earlier attempts at keeping a daily spiritual practice, I mistakenly focused on a set ritual of shoulds: I should read the Bible . . . I should pray every day . . . and it should look like thus and so. This limited approach did not engage all the chambers of my heart. I found myself unable to stick to what I thought I ought to be doing. Everything changed when I included all three parts in my spiritual discipline—coming to stillness, listening in quiet, and presenting my needs and desires in spoken prayer.

TASK: Consider if efforts you made in the past to keep a spiritual discipline were perhaps too narrow and engaged only a part of yourself. How might your practice now be supplemented with some of the approaches taught by Francis?

The time I spend doing a spiritual discipline allows me to go to that interior place where I experience calm, peace, and understanding of the moral and spiritual part of myself. For a brief time I move out of the secular, chaotic outside world. The reading I do has an influence on me that lasts on into the day. During a meeting or while working at my desk, I think of something I read that morning and quietly smile. I hope that remembering also makes me more sensitive to people around me. Part of my spiritual discipline is a promise to myself that during the day I will stop for short periods to be quiet, to reflect on the spiritual. This gives my work day better pace.

I participate in a group that practices the ancient form of sacred reading called *lectio divina*—reading with concentration and reflecting on questions like, "What was this writer like? What were the circumstances under which this was written? What is God telling me? What is the application of what I am reading to my own life?" We call it listening with the heart. Nobody ever told me in law school: "Listen with your heart." So I've had to learn how to do this. We meditate, using a centering word or phrase, connecting with that inner space where spirit and soul reside. Then I pray just as if I am in conversation. Nothing is too trivial to mention. All of this makes me conscious of the interiority of my life and I feel connected to God and am much more centered.

—R. K., attorney
and lobbyist

*Part Three*

✿

## Chapter Seven

# COMING TO STILLNESS

*The necessary thing is, after all, but
this: solitude, great inner solitude. Going
into oneself and . . . meeting no one—
this one must be able to attain.*

—*Rainer Maria Rilke*

"Pomp and Circumstance" at a high school graduation, the dimming of the lights in a theater, "The Star-Spangled Banner" at a ball game: what do these all have in common? They signal. They announce: Pay attention. Get ready. The event is starting. This initial music or action or event demarcates then—whatever was happening before—from now, when something else is about to begin.

One challenge of carrying out a daily spiritual practice is to find things that serve to separate this activity from everything we were doing before and are going to do afterwards. John Dunne, musician and theology professor from Notre Dame, knows this challenge well: "It is good," he urges, "to have some sort of structure or routine that jollies us along into prayer." But how do you turn off the ramble? Leave the regular? Step from squirming dailiness into the quiet? This is the time in our day to shift from focusing on the exterior happenings in our life, to focusing on the interior. What structures can we set up that will enable us to make this shift?

There are as many answers as there are people who speak; for any activity, any structure, can be entrance into silent and spoken prayer. Many are as simple as the single chime of a bell or the light of a solitary candle: "I am here. Attention is now being paid. Deep calls unto deep. With this act I signal and mark this time from that." Other activities are more extensive: Listening to music, making art, preparing a gratitude list, reading and studying, writing. These structures—and dozens more would work as well—serve to take us inward where we can witness and observe our interior life as prelude to silent and spoken prayer.

## USING MUSIC

The use of music in this initial phase of our daily spiritual discipline takes many forms. A friend told me about listening to Bach's "Little Fugue in G Minor" as part of that day's spiritual discipline.

> *As I was listening I thought about being in conversation with God, and I was struck by how much this piece of music mirrors my relationship with God. When I first began conversing with God, it was very simple, like the opening of the Fugue. In reply, God did not repeat my melody but responded in a harmonic way, just as Bach has his instruments do. Over time, our conversation—the Divine's and mine—has built in richness, complexity, depth and beauty, like the fugue builds. Ebb and flow occur in the dynamics of both the music and my communication with God, but my soul is constantly stirred by the heartbreaking beauty of what I hear and what I know.*

Music is clearly an opening for her into the Eternal.

Music has been used as part of worship and prayer for hundreds, perhaps thousands, of years. Think of chant, canticle, antiphon, hymn, plainsong, psalmody, and anthem, just to name a few of the forms music takes in celebrating the human connecting with the Divine and the celebration that comes from that connection. Sacred music operates in a different kind of time from ordinary experience and suggests the continuity of ritual performed regularly through centuries. We can listen to Aretha Franklin and Al Green testify; to the Anonymous Four and Vox bring medieval canticles into the present; to the Morman Tabernacle Choir and George Beverly Shea sound out anthems. Used as part of our daily spiritual discipline, music can summon a different quality of energy and prepare us for sitting in silence and praying our vocal prayers.

## USING ART

Until a few years ago I would never have imagined myself using art as an entrance into anything, especially a daily spiritual practice. In third grade art period, mine was the only cottonball-box horse with pipe-cleaner legs that wouldn't stand up. From that moment on, I knew I could not "do art."

But, fortunately, I discovered collage. This art form, thank goodness, is accessible even to the amateur and I find myself using it frequently to begin my daily spiritual practice. Collage—first tearing out a variety of images or using found objects from many sources and then putting them together to make a new image—not only takes me to my interior, it also symbolizes—usually long before I experience such a reality inside me—the possibility of the fragments of my self being united into a new pattern, a new whole.

I found a paragraph in Anne Truitt's *Daybook: The Journal of an Artist* that associated art and spiritual practice in an interesting way. The sculptor was asked where she thought art came from, from what part of the mind:

*I answered that I did not know but I thought it possible to put one's self in the way of art much in the same way that cloistered devotees place themselves in the way of religious experience. Art comes, if we are blessed with what Jack Tworkov called a "little touch of grace," into the highest part of the mind, that with which we can know the presence of God. But we have to pay attention to that area in order to notice the grace, or even perhaps to attract it.*

"But we have to pay attention," Anne Truitt says. That is what an activity like making a collage (or drawing, knitting, painting a picture, throwing clay, making a quilt square, playing with finger paints—anything that we experience as artful) contributes to our daily spiritual practice. We start to attend to something that reflects or illumines our interior state and, by so doing, we have put ourselves in the way of grace—"to notice the grace, or even perhaps to attract it."

## HILDEGARD OF BINGEN

There was a fascinating woman who lived in West Franconia, Germany, at the beginning of the twelfth century whose approach to practicing the spiritual life integrated music and art in a way that can be an inspiration to anyone who is inclined to begin a spiritual discipline with music or art.

Hildegard of Bingen would be thought of today as phenomenal for any one of a number of accomplishments. Born to noble parents, she became an abbess, spiritual counselor, physician (making unique contributions to gynecology), writer, reformer, preacher, and artist. She wrote two treatises on medicine and natural history, reflecting a quality of scientific observation rare in the early 1100s. She wrote a major scientific and medical encyclopedia that included a comprehensive herbal directory, a bestiary, and a lapidary. Her *Book of Compound Medicine: Causes and Cures* was considered a handbook of diseases and their remedies. She also, for her own amusement, contrived her own language. She went on four extended preaching tours; founded two monasteries; wrote six major books; argued ecclesiastical matters; advised popes, emperors, and princes who sought her wisdom because she was considered brilliant in matters of politics, church, and state; prophesied; healed the sick; painted; wrote poetry and composed music (she was the only twelfth century writer who composed hymns and sequences in free verse); and lived to be eighty years of age, dying in 1178.

When Hildegard recorded the visions of divine revelation which she began receiving at an early age, she included music and art in an integral way. Seeing images, hearing harmonies, and receiving words were all part of one experience for her: "Then I saw the brightest light in which I . . . heard various kinds of music . . . and [heard] a voice . . . (that) spoke as follows. . . ." She used paintings of images she saw in her visions to illustrate her books. She composed many pieces of music (much of which has been recorded by many artists in the last fifteen to twenty years). To read one of her spiritual poems or listen to one of her musical compositions (such as the lilting "Feather on the Breath of God") is to be as illumined by art and inspired by music as it is to be taught by the text.

## USING READING

There are those for whom books are an open door, a friendly hand, a beneficent guide, a beckoning adventure. One of the best ways for such individuals to enter daily quiet time is to read. Many focus on a sacred text like the Bible or the Torah, finding entrance into daily quiet time through the poetry of the Psalms or the stories of the Exodus, the parables of the Gospels or the stories of the life of Jesus. Some like classic spiritual texts like Dame Julian's *Revelations of Divine Love* or Brother Lawrence's *Practicing the Daily Presence of God.* Some like contemporary offerings such as Roberta Bondi's *To Pray and to Love* or George Gallup and Timothy Jones' *The Saints Among Us: How the Spiritually Committed Are Changing Our World.*

Some delve into writers whose works have helped shape the spiritual sensibilities of the twentieth century: writers like Henri Nouwen, Thomas Merton, Etty Hillesum, Martin Buber, Evelyn Underhill, Dietrich Bonhoeffer, Elizabeth Johnson. One of my friends finds much room for spiritual thoughts in the poems of Emily Dickinson and the novels of Frederich Bechner.

What wealth of images spiritual books can provide! I think of Dame Julian of Norwich, like Hildegard of Bingen, another phenomenal woman in the history of spiritual matters. A contemporary of Chaucer, Dame Julian, also known as Dame Juliana, was the author of *Revelations of Divine Love,* which has been referred to as the first book of theology written in English. Though she called herself a "simple creature unlearned," her writings are, according to the *Encyclopedia Brittanica,* "unparalleled in English religious literature. . . . The clarity and depth of her perception, the precision and accuracy of her theological presentation, and the sincerity and beauty of her expression reveal a mind and personality of exceptional strength and charm."

Many researchers believe Dame Julian, who may have been a Benedictine nun, was actively involved in founding schools for poor girls and boys. She established herself in a hermitage room attached to the cathedral in Norwich, England, where she lived for much of her adult life. A window on one side of Dame Julian's room looked out into the church, and the window on another side opened onto the road where traders were passing constantly. (Norwich was then the second largest city in England and the largest port.) Dame Julian, with her cat on her shoulder, perhaps—for we know she had a cat—would open her window and provide spiritual advice and counseling to anyone who came asking, leading at least one twentieth-century writer to call her affectionately the first "drive-by spiritual counselor."

Here is Dame Julian's amazing insight, recorded in her book *Revelations of Divine Love* (remember, it was 1373!):

> *God showed me in my palm a little thing round as a ball about the size of a hazelnut. I looked at it with the eye of my understanding and asked myself: 'What is this thing?' And I was answered: 'It is everything that is created.' I wondered how it could survive since it seemed so little it could suddenly disintegrate into nothing. The answer came: 'It endures and ever will endure, because God loves it.' And so everything has being because of God's love.*

There is also Dame Julian's famous image of God in a point. "In my understanding I saw God in a point. In seeing this I saw that God is in all things. God works in creatures because God is in the mid-point of everything and does all that is done. . . ."

Moving forward three hundred years, we come to another writer whose simple yet exuberant words readers relish today as a means by which they settle into quiet. Brother Lawrence, known as an awkward fellow who broke everything, was a footman and soldier before he joined the barefooted Carmellite order in Paris in 1666. As a lay brother, he spent much of his time working in the kitchen where he experienced God as easily while he cooked or brought in stove wood as another person might, bowing before a cathedral altar.

Listen to the down-to-earth spiritual ideas of Brother Lawrence captured in his little tome which is today considered a classic, *The Practice of the Presence of God*: "And it is not necessary to have great things to do. I turn my little omelet in the pan for the love of God . . . When I cannot do anything else, it is enough for me to have lifted a straw from the earth for the love of God."

I like his sense of humor: "The enclosed is an answer to that which I received from _____; pray deliver it to her. She seems to me full of good will, but she would go faster than grace. One does not become holy all at once."

And his equanimity amazes: "The time of business does not with me differ from the time of prayer, and in the noise and clatter of my kitchen, while several persons are at the same time calling for different things, I possess God in as great tranquillity as if I were upon my knees at the blessed sacrament."

For thousands of years readers have started their spiritual practice by reading in The Psalms. I know this is one of the quickest and surest ways for me to start to exchange the harum-scarum of my daily living for a space of the still and the eternal. The gaggle of folk who wrote these prayers which take the form of temple entrance songs, poems, school exercises, and cries from the heart knew human nature. I find the circumstances of my life all through the one hundred and fifty Psalms.

Here I am feeling sorry for myself:

*I pour out my complaints . . . I tell my trouble . . . nobody cares for me.*

—*Psalm 142*

Here I am angry at somebody:

*God, show her how it feels!*

—*Psalm 109*

Here I am, borne up by the sheer beauty of poetry:

*My heart is steadfast, O God, my heart is steadfast! I will sing*
*and make melody! Awake my soul! Awake, O harp and lyre!*
*I will awake the dawn!*

*—Psalm 108*

When I am grieving, I find:

*O Lord, my heart is not lifted up, my eyes are not raised too high*
*. . . But I have calmed and quieted my soul like a child quieted*
*at its mother's breast; like a child that is quieted is my soul.*

*—Psalm 131*

When a bad time is finally over, I relax with:

*We have escaped as a bird from the snare of the fowlers; the*
*snare is broken, and we have escaped! Our help is in the name*
*of the Lord, who made heaven and earth.*

*—Psalm 124*

When I need assurance:

*You shall eat the fruit of the labour of your hands; you shall*
*be happy, and it shall be well with you.*

*—Psalm 128*

I find an answer for the perennial question, "Will my prayers
be answered?" when I read:

*On the day I called, thou didst answer me: my strength of soul*
*thou didst increase.*

*—Psalm 138*

## USING WRITING

Reading spiritual books and sacred scriptures provides a way to
shift from the surface and the immediate of our exterior lives to

questions of meaning and depth in our interior lives. Writing can do the same. People who would never consider themselves writers use writing to begin their daily spiritual discipline. A friend of mine who travels the world as president of her communications company explores specific spiritual questions in her writing: What does give meaning to my life? What is the right thing to do in this touchy situation? How shall I best teach my children about God? She reports that more than once, while she wrote, things have become clear. She is able to hear a different kind of wisdom.

Writing as the beginning activity for daily sacred quiet time can also take the form of putting entries into a journal. You will enjoy including in your journal entries like these: your response to passages from your sacred reading that inspire you, musings about spiritual subjects and questions important to you, and the recounting of dreams that intrigue you. You might make lists: Ten Things Important to My Inner Life, Nineteen Reasons Quiet Time and Prayer are Worth the Effort, Five Sacred Places I Want to Visit, Things I Would Do If I Were In Charge of the World, Spiritual Figures I Would Like to Meet, and any other kind of list that strikes your fancy.

You might write imaginary conversations with spiritual figures—people like Mother Teresa; John Wesley; famous women in the Old Testament like Ruth, Naomi, and Esther; Francis of Assisi and his partner Sister Clare; Moses or his sister Miriam; famous women in the New Testament like Mary, Elizabeth, Mary Magdalene, Lydia, Martha and her sister Mary, Priscilla. You can write prayers and compose poems and songs. You can keep a dated record of specific requests you make in prayer and how these prayers are answered, whether over time or immediately. You can write letters to God.

One of the most valuable things you can do in your journal is to keep adding to your spiritual autobiography by remembering moments, events, and situations when you felt connected to the sacred. Describe what happened; delineate the lasting impact of these holy encounters. When you feel distant and separated from God, which happens to everyone at some time or other, you can re-read the accounts in your spiritual autobiography. No one can dispute the value or power of these events. You can say, "I experienced them. No one nor nothing can take these sacred encounters away. I was there. I know. I remember."

Often insights jump off the page as you write. Or you think of something you have never thought of before. A new thing emerges. Wisdom and guidance show up on the page. William Stafford, a poet and teacher whom I was privileged to have as a friend, helped me understand this power of writing many years ago:

> *Writers are not so much people who have something to say as they are people who have found a process that will bring about new things they would not have thought of if they had not started to say them . . . the possibilities are endless. If I put down something, that thing will help the next thing come, and I'm off. If I let the process go on, things will occur to me that were not at all in my mind when I started. These things, odd or trivial as they may be, are somehow connected. And if I let them string out, surprising things will happen.*

When you let writing happen, like Bill Stafford suggests, as part of your daily spiritual discipline, you fulfill an important vocation—finding out what the world is trying to be. Your world. Your inner and your outer world.

## USING A COMMONPLACE BOOK

In addition to journal writing, I have used another method that involves some writing and some collecting to begin my daily spiritual practice. I keep a large (11x14 inch), inexpensive, spiral-bound sketch book (I get these at the art supply store) which I call my Commonplace Book.

Years ago, when I taught writing to college students, I came across a piece of interesting information about the Greeks. It seems that the Greeks had a practice of copying down bits of conversation they heard, quotes they read, excerpts that struck them, their own thoughts on particular matters. A book of such personal compilations the Greeks felt could—and did—actually form a person's character. I adapted this Greek idea to my own life by keeping a book in which I not only wrote my own journal entries, dreams, and dialogues, but where I put newspaper excerpts that struck me, quotations I came across, verses from Scripture that spoke to me, poems, pictures.

As I pick up my current Commonplace Book, I notice the entries that illustrate the continuing unfolding of my spiritual life in my daily practice. On one page is an article from the *New York Times* about a renowned artist of the early 20th century, Marsden Hartley, for whom painting mountains was a way of seeking the spiritual. "Few of nature's offerings," the article says, "moved Marsden Hartley quite so much as mountains. . . . For him, they were symbols of permanence and aspiration, but they had a deeper significance, too. 'I know I have seen God now,' he wrote to a friend in 1939 after a camping trip to Mount Katahdin, Maine's highest peak."

Across the page from this article on art in my Commonplace Book, I have a piece, again from the *New York Times,* titled "Grand Examples of the Right Stuff for Aging Well." More and more I am keenly aware of the integral relationship between the physical body and the Spirit contained and held by the body.

As I page through the Commonplace Book, I see a thank-you card from my sister Barbara and a letter from my brother Frank . . . love showing up as family connection.

I see a two-page color spread of Mesa Verde, the cliff-dwelling home of the ancient Anasazi . . . definitely a spiritual place for me.

The Commonplace Book also has a couple obituaries of people that I did not know but whose epitaphs reveal they lived life doing the things for which they had passion.

The first . . . "J. Blan van Urk, a high-spirited sportsman and sometimes public relations man, author and entrepreneur who spent the better part of a century riding happily to the hounds, died on Monday . . . He was 95 and a widely recognized authority on fox hunting and lunch."

And the second . . . "C. G. Sontheimer, Cuisinart Backer, dies at 83. . . . he was known as the man who revolutionized American cooking by bringing Cuisinart to the United States. . . . it's a shudder to think what would have happened—or not happened—to American cooking if Mr. Sontheimer had taken up golf."

I am inspired by these men's commitment to do the things for which they had passion.

There are also many journal entries, copies of e-mail from friends, one drawing I made of some images from a dream, several verses from the Bible with my comments, and on and on. I've discovered such a form of writing and compiling allows me to notice what I pay attention to, gives me time and space to contemplate this collection, and reveals threads of continuity, areas of concern, and textures in inner and outer life.

Joseph Campbell once said:

> *You must have a room or a certain hour of the day or so where you do not know what was in the morning paper, where you do not know who your friends are, you don't know what you owe anybody, or what they owe you—but a place where you can simply experience and bring forth what you are, and what*

*you might be . . . At first you may find nothing's happening.
. . . But if you have a sacred place and use it, take advantage
of it, something will happen.*

So whether it's for one minute, two minutes or sixty . . .
whether it's knitting or needlepoint, writing or painting, listening to music or watching the birds, reading sacred Scripture or
lighting a candle . . . whatever can bring us to stillness, that is
what we need to do.

## REFLECTION

*What can you do to find great inner solitude, going into yourself . . .
meeting no one, as the poet Rilke urges in the quotation that opens
this chapter?*

## SACRED TASKS

One step at a time, even the smallest of steps, can move you
amazingly far down the path of establishing a period of daily
sacred quiet time. When I began, I spent less than five minutes.
My opening activity was to sit down. My period of quiet was
about the amount of time it took me to say the *Lord's Prayer* in
my head a few times. (Someone has estimated that you can get
through the *Lord's Prayer* in about twenty seconds.) My spoken
prayer was one or two sentences.

I have a friend who began her spiritual discipline by using a
three-minute egg timer. This person hated to be still and didn't
like silence. But she wanted to have a daily spiritual practice that
brought her serenity and peace. So she stuck it out for three
minutes . . . and today she could, I think, inspire a brick to start
a spiritual discipline.

TASK: Consider what first small steps you can take to begin a daily spiritual discipline. What appeals to you the most? Do any of the entrance activities discussed in this chapter interest you? What is the thing that most serves to quiet you? How can this activity become part of your daily spiritual discipline? Thinking about questions like these can help quick-start your own version of daily quiet time and prayer.

When you start a daily spiritual discipline, you discover early on that life doesn't just bend itself toward quiet and solitude. You have to do something that gives shape to your inner world.

TASK: Consider what kind of place and what kind of activity would help you move into solitude. How can you go about making this place and activity a reality? Can you begin one of your ideas today or tomorrow?

I keep a spiritual discipline because it nurtures me. Particularly on the dark days when I am having difficulty with someone or something in my life. My practice consists of a twenty-minute silent meditation called Centering Prayer, which helps me keep my balance and the perspective that "this too shall pass." On the good days when I feel overpowered with God's blessings in my life, the spiritual practice gives me a place to acknowledge gifts I certainly did not earn.

My spiritual discipline provides a place where I don't have to have all the right answers. A place where it is safe for me to see and admit my faults and failures and have that recognition contribute something to who I am rather than have it diminish me. I grow as a result, and that seems to make it worth whatever pain I may feel in confronting my shortcomings.

For a long time, I struggled because I thought a spiritual discipline had to be done "right." But I found that trying to do it right got in the way of doing it at all. Rarely does it look like what I used to think it should look like. What I focus on now is being consistent in keeping the practice, not on how well I'm doing it. One amusing outcome of this consistency is, now that I've done the practice enough over the years, I find that if I decide to take an afternoon nap, I always wake up after twenty minutes, the same length of time I typically spend in Centering Prayer!

—A. O., president
of a non-profit foundation

# Chapter Eight

## LISTENING IN QUIET

*Quiet minds cannot be perplexed or*
*frightened but go on in fortune or*
*misfortune at their own private pace, like*
*a clock during a thunderstorm.*

—Robert Louis Stevenson

I have always laughed at the story of Madame de Stael (her biography identifies her as a French-Swiss woman of letters, political propagandist, and conversationalist who lived at the time of the French Revolution). It seems that on one particular occasion Madame de Stael spent two hours with a friend and never stopped talking once. As she left, she reportedly said to the friend, who had not gotten a word in during the entire visit, "What a delightful conversation we have had!"

I laugh because I've prayed like this many a time. "Help me with this; please do that; here is what is needed, Lord; ad infinitum . . . An entirely one-sided conversation. I do all the talking; God, I'm expecting, will do all the listening.

The truth is, I didn't know there was any other way to pray until I was well into adulthood. I did not know about the kind of praying one does in silence, where the object is to listen, not to talk. And when I did discover this ancient form of prayer and tried to practice it, I became an instant failure.

## THE CHALLENGE OF SITTING IN SILENCE

Sit still and keep my mind focused on some word or passage and experience calmness and quiet? You have to be kidding. As soon as I sat down, I thought of a dozen emergencies—my car needed new anti-freeze (and the month was July); I had to call my college roommate (whom I hadn't talked to for twenty years); the newspaper was still out on the lawn and might get wet (though the morning was bright and sunny).

I felt better when I came across the Chinese teacher Wu Ch'eng-en's tongue-in-cheek confession:

> *If it were just a matter of playing football with the firmament, stirring up the ocean, turning back rivers, carrying away mountains, seizing the moon, moving the Pole-star or shifting a planet, I could manage it easily enough . . . But if it comes to sitting still and meditating, I am bound to come off badly. It's quite against my nature to sit still.*

It is reassuring to know I am not the only person who has ever felt remedial in the quiet prayer department. Becoming distracted by jumbled and unpredictable thoughts seems to be an integral part of trying to be quiet. When we become still, we hear all the internal racket. Our minds are like the car radio that cuts in and out, that picks up first this frequency and then that frequency on an isolated stretch of road. The thoughts are all the parts of our inner life, clamoring to be heard.

## THE PLEASURES OF SITTING IN SILENCE

The paradox related to this difficulty of sitting still and being quiet is, of course, that we also treasure silence. That is why many of us camp deep in the forest or go out into the desert to look at the stars or sail into an isolated cove or sit on the deck early in the morning with a cup of coffee—we love the quiet. Some part of us knows we are refreshed and stilled by whatever is contained in this precious silence. We understand the "sacrament of pause." We have all experienced it.

It is to take such experiences of quiet in our lives—which are often sporadic and always far too infrequent—and recreate and enlarge their value that we practice daily quiet time as part of our spiritual practice. By being quiet, we find the place inside us where our greatest authenticity dwells, where we are most who we are and who we want to be. In silence, we find our own center, but, most importantly, we also find the presence of the Holy Other.

## EXPERIENCING THE DIVINE IN THE SILENCE

Anthony Bloom, a medical doctor who later became an Eastern Orthodox priest, tells a story about finding the Divine in the quiet that I have never forgotten. Shortly after his ordination, Bloom was sent to conduct a service at a home for the elderly. A woman requested some advice about prayer. When he asked what problem she was having with her prayer, she replied that for fourteen years she had been saying her prayers a certain way and had never once in all that time perceived God's presence. Bloom replied to the woman, "If you speak all the time, you don't give God a chance to get a word in."

Then he gave her new instructions.

She was to go to her room, place her armchair in a position where the dark corners of her room were behind her, and light a lamp. "Just sit," he said, "look round, and try to see where you live, because I am sure that if you have prayed all these

fourteen years it is a long time since you have seen your room.
And then," he added, "take your knitting and for fifteen minutes knit before the face of God." But she was not to say one
word of prayer. "You just knit and try to enjoy the peace of
your room."

The woman didn't think this was very pious advice, but
she tried it. Sometime later, when she saw Bloom again, she
told him, "You know, it works." He asked, "What works?
What happened?"

She told him that she had started off the experiment by
saying:

> *Oh, how nice. I have fifteen minutes during which I can do
> nothing without being guilty! . . . I felt so quiet because the
> room was so peaceful. There was a clock ticking but it didn't dis-
> turb the silence; its ticking just underlined the fact that every-
> thing was so still and after a while I remembered that I must
> knit before the face of God, and so I began to knit. . . . Then
> I perceived that this silence was not simply an absence of noise,
> but that the silence had substance. It was not absence of some-
> thing but presence of something. The silence had a density, a
> richness, and it began to pervade me. The silence around began
> to come and meet the silence in me.*

The woman paused in her story for several seconds. Then
she added, "All of a sudden I perceived that the silence was a
presence. At the heart of the silence there was One who is all
stillness, all peace, all poise."

The woman for the next (and last) ten years of her life—she
died at age a hundred and two—practiced both kinds of prayer,
the still silence and her previous vocal prayer. She was like the
old peasant, Bloom suggested, who when the priest asked him
why he spent hours and hours sitting in the chapel motionless,

doing nothing, answered: "I look at the Divine, the Divine looks at me, and we are happy."

## WAYS INTO SILENCE

But what is our way into this Silence, I ask myself, given my jumping-bean mind and my always-need-to-be-doing way of living? Fortunately, a lot of people have suggestions to make. We'll look at just four of the possibilities.

## POSSIBILITY ONE

John Main first learned the inner path of Silence from a holy Indian teacher. Later, after Main became a Benedictine monk, he found one day in the writings of John Cassian, a Catholic spiritual leader from the eighth century, a method of silent prayer. John Main was astonished to see that Cassian's suggestions were like the ones he had been taught years earlier by the holy man in India. Following this discovery, John Main's mission became to teach this method of prayer, which he had found in both eastern and western religions, a mission he remained dedicated to until his death in the early 1980s and which is carried on today by spiritual teachers such as Laurence Freeman.

Here is John Main's approach to listening in silence:

*What is the teaching? Sit down. Sit still. Close your eyes lightly. Sit relaxed but alert. Silently, interiorly begin to say a single word. . . . (This word might be Love, Peace, Quiet, a Holy Name . . . John Main recommends the word "Maranatha," which means "Come, Lord" in Aramaic.) Listen to the word as you say it, gently but continuously. Do not think*

*or imagine anything—spiritual or otherwise. If thoughts
and images come, these are distractions at the time of meditation, so keep returning to the simple work of saying the
word. Meditate between twenty and thirty minutes each
morning and evening.*

## POSSIBILITY TWO

This approach to listening in silence is called Centering Prayer.
It is similar to John Main's approach, except the word you choose
is repeated only when your mind wanders, not continuously.
Here are simple instructions:

> *First of all, we settle ourselves down quietly. Most of us pray
> best sitting down, but take any posture that works well for you.
> It is best if the back is fairly straight and well supported. If we
> gently close our eyes, we immediately begin to quiet down, for
> we use a lot of our psychic energy in seeing.*
>
> *Once we are settled, we turn our attention to the Lord pres-
> ent within us. In love we turn ourselves over to the Divine. In
> order to be able to abide quietly and attentively with the Divine,
> we use a prayer word—a simple word that expresses our being
> to the Lord in love. This word might be a holy name or words
> like love, peace, mercy, silence, yes, amor, shalom, or amen. We
> just let that word be there.*
>
> *Whenever, during the time of our prayer, we become aware
> of anything else, we simply use our word to return to prayer.
> Some days we will have to use the word constantly. Other days
> we may not need to use our word much at all. It really makes
> no difference.*
>
> *At the end of twenty minutes, we end our prayer very gen-
> tly, perhaps praying interiorly, very slowly, a prayer like Our*

*Father or perhaps a Psalm. Or merely remain in silence with
eyes closed for a couple of minutes. Then expect the effects of
the prayer—love, joy, peace, kindness—to occur in your daily
life, not in the period of Centering Prayer itself. Centering
Prayer is a relationship with God and a discipline to foster
that relationship. It habituates us to the language of God
which is silence.*

## POSSIBILITY THREE

This third approach to listening in silence comes from Eknath
Easwaran, who first came to America from India as a Fulbright
Professor of English. His common-sense approach to quiet
prayer is used by thousands of individuals from many cultures,
practicing many creeds. In fact, it was Professor Easwaran's suggestions that I followed when I first began my spiritual discipline, and I continue to use my own version of his method today
as one way I structure my quiet time.

Here are this teacher's instructions:

He recommends beginning with the Prayer of Saint Francis
of Assisi. He goes on to suggest that any passage you already
know, like the Twenty-third Psalm or some other will also do
nicely. Easwaran also points out the words "Lord" and "Master"
in St. Francis' prayer are to be interpreted not as some white-
bearded gentleman ruling from a throne but as the very ground
of existence, the most profound thing we can conceive of. The
prayer of St. Francis goes like this:

*Lord, make me an instrument of thy peace.*
*Where there is hatred, let me sow love;*
*Where there is injury, pardon;*
*Where there is doubt, faith;*

*Where there is despair, hope;*
*Where there is darkness, light;*
*Where there is sadness, joy.*
*O divine Master, grant that I may not so much seek*
*To be consoled as to console,*
*To be understood as to understand,*
*To be loved as to love;*
*For it is in giving that we receive;*
*It is in pardoning that we are pardoned;*
*It is in dying (to self) that we are born to eternal life.*

You repeat this prayer, seated with eyes closed. The repetition is done word by word, very slowly. (Whatever your pace, Easwaran suggests, let the words be comfortably spaced with elbow room between.) When distractions occur—as they most certainly will—follow this rule which you repeat to your mind: "I'm sorry, but if you run away from the passage, you will have to go back to the beginning and start again." Carry out this spiritual practice for thirty minutes.

I have talked with people who have followed Professor Easwaran's recommendations for twenty years or more, using the St. Francis Prayer, the Lord's Prayer, the Twenty-third Psalm, the Beatitudes and other passages they have memorized. Some days, they say, they do nothing else but bring their minds back to the beginning of the passage, over and over, again and again. This has certainly happened to me; and, when it does, I take enormous comfort in the centuries-old reassurance of another master of prayer, Francis de Sales: "Even if you do nothing during the whole of your hour but bring your mind back and place it again in our Lord's presence, though it went away every time you brought it back, your hour would be very well employed."

## POSSIBILITY FOUR

Another approach to listening in silence is to watch the breath. A friend of mine who has followed this method for several decades as a way to sit in quiet offers these words:

> I do a few yoga postures before getting started. This connects me to my body. Then I say a few times the phrase: Be still and know that the I Am who is both without and within me is God. Next, I concentrate on my breathing. I recognize my breath as the breath of God; I think of the story of God breathing into the form of clay and the clay becoming a living person. I think of the breath as the Spirit flowing within me, regenerating me. I actually visualize this breath moving to every cell and my body dancing with light. This brings a sense of relaxation. I become very conscious of the breath I breathe every minute and connect this breath to the Spirit of God. I watch my breath for a few minutes; and then I conclude my practice with a list of gratitudes and perhaps writing insights or thoughts in my journal.

## ALERTNESS IN SILENCE

Anthony Bloom talks about the kind of alertness you need when you sit in silence. It is, he says, like bird watching—which implies stillness, quiet and repose and, at the same time, intense alertness because "if you sit in the fields dreaming the undreamt dreams of your short night all the birds will have gone along before you realize that the sun is warming your back." It is the kind of alertness that allows you to have an open mind, free from prejudice or expectation, so you can receive the impact of anything that comes your way.

Theophane the Recluse, an early monastic leader, speaking of the way in which people usually think, says that thoughts buzz around in our heads like a swarm of mosquitoes, in all directions, monotonously, without order and without particular results. By sitting in silence, the thing you are creating, by using a word or a passage, is a kind of coherence. Whenever you begin to think of things divine, all kinds of subsidiary thoughts start to appear. By choosing the subject of your thinking—a word or a passage—or by watching your breathing, you have an organizing principle that can hold your thoughts so your listening can come from the deep.

## REPETITION IN THE SILENCE

But what about all this repetition? John Main's approach of repeating a word continuously, Centering Prayer's approach of choosing a prayer word and returning to it when the mind wanders, Eknath Easwaran's teaching of the repetition of a complete passage like a prayer or scripture; my friend watching her breath in and out, in and out. Isn't this monotony at its worst? The very kind of vain repetitions that Jesus himself said would never be heard?

I once read what theatrical director Peter Brook had to say about the act of repetition. Actors, of course, repeat and repeat as they rehearse. What he says is happening when an actor recites the same lines over and over and over is that the repetition allows the meaning of the role and the message of the theme to penetrate the actor's character. This coming back again and again, Brook says, allows time to enter as a progressive force; repeating the same actions enables the penetration to go deeper. This allows barriers to understanding, false notions, and confusions to fall away.

Actors, the director says, can come to the repetition of their practice of the play in one of two ways. They can approach the repetition mechanically, which will mean they are put to sleep by it. Or they can bring themselves to the repetition in such a way they are challenged by it; and the challenge itself will awaken whatever is latent in them that is needed for them to become the role they are about to play on the stage.

Director Brook's understanding of the value and impact of actors' repetition of words and phrases applies to any one of the four approaches to silent prayer. This coming back again and again allows time to enter as a progressive force, and repeating enables the truths to penetrate deeper. Because no two periods of quiet are exactly the same, it is, as the poet Gertrude Stein said, very much like a frog hopping. The frog cannot ever hop exactly the same distance or exactly the same way at every hop. No matter how often you repeat something, if there is anything alive in the repeating, the emphasis is different.

So the answer to any possible boredom and numbing repetition is our aliveness and alertness when we sit in silence. (Remember Brook's assertion that the actors could either bring deadness or aliveness to the repetition of their lines.) If you see the passage or word as a challenge to be engaged with, using the kind of alertness Anthony Bloom suggests a bird watcher has—still, quiet, yet very awake—the meaning of the experience will become more and more an integrated part of who you are.

## THE CONTRIBUTIONS OF SILENCE

The Jewish mystical writings known as the Kabbalah tell us solitude is the domain of the soul, and the soul is a portion of God that resides in our bodies. It is in solitude, in silence, the Kabbalah suggests, that the soul has its greatest chance to grow.

Mother Teresa certainly knew about the soul needing silence. A reporter once asked her how she could do all she did, taking care of the sick and dying, year in, year out. Mother

Teresa answered that she started every day sitting in silence and adoration before the altar for one hour. Then she added, "The more we receive in silent prayer, the more we can give in our active life. We need to find God, and God cannot be found in noise and restlessness. We need silence to touch souls."

What can you expect from this time of sitting in silence?

The anonymous fourteenth-century author of *Cloud of Unknowing* says it may seem at times that nothing is happening:

> *Your bodily wits may find there nothing to feed on. They think that you are doing nothing. Still keep on doing this nothing—provided you do it for love of God. Cease not but travail busily in that nothing with a conscious desire to want to have God. . . . I tell you truly, I would rather be in this nowhere place, blindly wrestling with nothing than to be some great lord who could go where he wanted to and amuse himself with anything he liked.*

If you persist in the nothing, gradual, almost imperceptible changes begin to happen in your life. It's like the weavers in India who meditate on their design before putting their hand to the loom. They sit still in mediation for a few minutes before beginning the work. When asked why, the weavers say, "Without being silent for a while, it is not wise to start one's work. The design will elude one's fingers if one's mind is tinged with unrest."

## MANY CULTURES
## AND THE VALUE OF LISTENING IN SILENCE

The value—and necessity—of this listening prayer of quiet is recorded in many cultures. I read statements like the ones below and wonder, "How could I ever be so shortsighted as not to take advantage of something recognized universally as a path to wisdom and as a way to connect to the peace of my very soul?"

Let's listen to just a few voices from across the centuries and around the globe:

An anonymous monk living in the Egyptian desert in the 600s:

*Unless there is a still center in the middle of the storm, unless individuals in the midst of all their activities preserve a secret room in their hearts where they sit alone before God, unless we do this, we will lose all sense of spiritual direction and be torn to pieces.*

The Indian poet Kabir:

*I laugh when I hear that the fish in the water is thirsty. Perceivest thou not how the god is in thine own house, that thou wanderest from forest to forest so listlessly? In thy home is the Truth. Go where thou wilt, to Benares or to Mathura; if thy soul is a stranger to thee, the whole world is unhomely.*

The Chinese philosopher Lao Tzu:

*There is no need to run outside for better seeing. Nor to peer from a window. Rather abide at the center of your being; for the more you leave it, the less you learn. Search your heart and see if he is wise who takes each turn; the way to do is to be. The answer was always quietly there, only our questions drowned it out.*

Attributed to the Buddha:

*Don't just do something; stand there.*

From Judaism and Christianity, the Psalm:

*Be still, and know that I am God.*

From Jesus:

*When you pray, go into a room by yourself, shut the door, and pray.*

Reading these examples about the importance of silence, examples that cross cultures and time, I'm reminded of an old saying that goes something like: "I always take fifteen minutes for praying in silence every day unless I've got too many pressing situations. Then I take thirty." I hope I can learn to be such a wise person.

It has been suggested that God keeps a layer of silence between human beings and the Mystery and that we must also keep a silence in which to approach that Mystery. The Divine is a self-giving Silence, pouring into us. That Silence, in turn, makes us articulate to ourselves and to the world. You and I are made for this listening prayer. It is the most human and personal thing we can do.

## REFLECTION

*Can you recall a time that you heard the silence?*
*What would you speculate moves us about silence?*

## SACRED TASK

Two friends came for lunch the other day, and we were talking about listening to the Divine in silence. One friend remarked, "You know, a lot of people are frightened of silence. They are very fearful of what they might find there. What if something gets them, catches them; what if they were to uncover something that they didn't want to deal with?"

My other friend, who has practiced a daily spiritual discipline for almost fifty years, responded: "Fear is a major characteristic of the world we live in; many of us exist in fear. But in quiet there is the possibility of a moment or moments of freedom from that fear. That's the beauty of having a spiritual discipline. For that period of time, you can be free of fear!"

The conversation reminded me about the basket a spiritual director once told me to imagine. She suggested whenever I begin my quiet time I put all my fears, problems, and concerns in the imaginary basket. Then after I had listened in silence, the director said, I could take everything out of the basket and offer it to God as I prayed with words to end my spiritual discipline for that day.

TASK: Can you identify fears and concerns that might be barriers to listening in silence? You might experiment for a few weeks or a month or two with doing your spiritual practice anyway, in spite of these fears and concerns, and just see what happens.

The more hectic life becomes, the more my moorings slip if I don't consciously commit the day to God. This time of commitment is where I find the grounding for the day, where I recognize that God is sovereign and that I am not in control. I use a devotional book that has a journal included, and I write down thoughts and short prayers in it. Then I read one chapter in Proverbs, going along with the days of the month. (There are thirty-one chapters in the book.) Throughout this time I am, I hope, in a state of silent prayer, wanting God to live through me this day. Then I may read other chapters in the Bible, closing in spoken prayer.

In case this sounds very "religious," let it be known that I fight going back to sleep, my wandering mind, and wanting to do other things. However, over the years, I have found that more and more I look forward to (and need) this time. A wise woman once told me that God does not have favorites, but God does have intimates. I want to be an intimate of God's, and the only way I know to do that is spend time daily in my spiritual discipline.

—K. J. H., television talk show host

## Chapter Nine

### PRAYING WITH WORDS

*I don't know of a single foreign product
that enters this country untaxed, except
the answer to prayer.*

—Mark Twain

We bring our three-part spiritual discipline to a close by praying with words. When you sat in silence in the preceding part of
the practice of your spiritual discipline, you were listening. Waiting. Absorbing. Lingering. Now that you are moving into the
praying with words part of our practice, you are taking action.
Prayer is a vital transaction. When you pray, you engage in active
enterprise, in active interchange. Prayer is meeting life with Life
at its source and asking for changes to be made, for things to
happen, for good to be done, for right to prevail. Prayer is moving out into the world.

In praying with words, you speak your deepest thoughts and
concerns to a caring and compassionate listener. You hold a conversation with a listener with whom you are in the process every day
of building a cumulative life of friendship. During this time of praying with words, it's as if you are hanging out on the wash line, in the
presence of a friend, all the needs, desires, requests, problems, confusions—and on a good day, the joys and gratitudes—of your life.

It is good and it is appropriate that, by praying, you pay attention to all your wishes, hopes, disappointments, and fears. Authentic prayer encompasses every kind of speaking on every kind of subject. And you can take heart in knowing that prayer is prayer, no matter how limited or how broad the scope. The Divine does not care.

## HOW TO PRAY

I came across a piece once at a retreat that teaches, in a folksy kind of way, how to pray. The anonymous letter is written as if the Divine were speaking:

*Dear One Who Prays:*

*You do not have to be clever to please me. Just speak to me as you would to anyone of whom you are fond. Are there any people you want to pray for? Say their names to me, and ask of me as much as you like. I am generous, and know all their needs; but I want you to show your love for them and me by trusting me to do what I know is best.*

*Tell me about the poor, the sick, and the troubled; and, if you have lost the friendship or affection of anyone, tell me about that too. Is there anything you want for your soul? If you like, you can write out a long list of all your needs and come read it to me. Tell me of the things you feel guilty about. I will forgive you if you will accept it. Tell me about your pride, your touchiness, self-centeredness, meanness, and laziness. I still love you in spite of these. Do not be ashamed. There are many saints in heaven who had the same faults as you; they prayed, and little by little, their faults were corrected.*

*Do not hesitate to ask me for blessings for the body and mind, for health, memory, success. I can give everything. I always do give everything needed, if you truly want it. What is it that you want today? Tell me, for I long to do you good. What are your plans? Tell me about them. Is there anyone you want to please? What do you want to do for them? Tell me about your failures, and I will show you the cause of them. What are your worries? Who has caused you pain? Tell me about it; and, if you will forgive those who hurt you, I will bless you. Are you afraid of anything? Have you any tormenting, unreasonable fears? Trust yourself to me. I am here. I see everything. I will not leave you.*

*Share your joys with me. Share your happiness. Tell me what has happened since yesterday to cheer and comfort you. Show me your gratitude and thank me.*

*Do you have peace of soul? If not, ask me and I will help you overcome the things that disturb you.*

*Well, go along now. Get on with your work or play or other interests. Try to be quieter, humbler, kinder; and come back soon and bring a devoted heart. Tomorrow I shall have more blessings for you.*

I personally am reassured by instructions like these and by unpretentious prayers like the one Thomas Merton prayed when he felt lost, without an inkling of what to do next in his life:

*My Lord God, I have no idea where I am going. I do not see the road ahead of me. I cannot know for certain where it will end. Nor do I really know myself, and the fact that I think I am following your will does not mean that I am actually doing so. But I believe that the desire to please you does in fact please you. And I hope I have this desire in all that I am doing. I hope that I never do anything apart from that desire. And I know that if I do this you will lead me by the right road though I may know nothing about it. Therefore, I will trust you always though I may seem to be lost and in the shadow of death. I will not fear, for you are ever with me, and you will never leave me to face my perils alone.*

I think when I read this prayer, "If Thomas Merton, a monk famous around the world for his brilliance, his spiritual teaching, his writings, needs on occasion to pray like this, then no wonder I bumble along, not knowing many times what to pray for."


## THE VARIETY OF WAYS PEOPLE PRAY

George Gallup, Jr., chairman of the George H. Gallup International Institute and well known for the polls associated with his name, talks about his life of prayer this way: "I like what Teresa of Avila said about prayer. 'The life of prayer is just the love of God and a liking to be with Him.' It means that prayer is . . . a substratum of life—a partnership with God . . . I use different prayers at different times . . . Through prayer I've seen a vision of what I believe God wants in my life."

The praying with which you complete your daily quiet time can be as simple as the one High Star, a Lakota Sioux singer, prays every morning: "Hi, God, give me a good day." It can be, as Martin Marty suggests, words of argument: "Why are you doing this?' Give me a fair shake." It can be a ritual like Carole Mu'min's Muslim prayer: "In the name of God, most gracious, most merciful. Praise be to God, the Cherisher and Sustainer of all the worlds . . . Thee do we worship and Thine aid we seek, Show us the straight way. . . ."

You can pray your pain: "Out of the depths I cry to you, O God, Hear my voice, O God, listen to my pleading." Your praying can be as light-hearted as the medieval invocation: "From ghoulies and ghosties and long-leggity beasties and things that go bump in the night, good Lord, deliver me." Your praying can be simple: "You are to me, O Lord, what wings are to the flying bird." No matter how and about what you pray on any specific day, you are speaking your desires, problems, fears, concerns, and joys in the presence of the Holy Other. You speak your authentic self. You converse.

## ANSWERS TO OUR PRAYERS

More times than not, you are praying for people you know—your children, parents, folks with whom you work, family members, friends—and for yourself. You pray for specific things—"Please let me get this new job; Take care of my boy as he grows to become a man; Help me find the money I need." You pray for changes in yourself—"Help me control my anger; Help me not to be so afraid; Heal me of this sickness." Wherever you are, whatever you need and want, whatever will make life more whole and fulfilled—all of this is appropriate content to be included in your conversation when you pray.

But then comes the rub.

If praying is conversing, you expect to get an answer. And what are you to think when the good you ask for doesn't happen, when the person you pray for doesn't get any better, when life seems to continue on in the same way? Have you failed as a pray-er? Is this whole idea one big hoax? Are you being silly—acting as if you are speaking to a caring Listener when what you are really doing is speaking into a canyon where all you hear is your own echo?

These are not idle questions. A survey was done a few years ago in which people who labeled themselves atheists and agnostics were asked what turned them toward this way of thinking. More cited unanswered prayers than any other explanation for their opinions.

I have heard this many times myself. "When I was twelve years old, I prayed for my daddy to get well," a neighbor of mine, close to retirement age, told me once, "and I really believed that the next morning when I got up he would be OK." She winced.

"The next morning he wasn't OK. The next morning he was dead. I haven't," she concluded, "believed in prayer since."

C. S. Lewis once said that every war, every famine, every death bed is a monument to some unanswered prayer. For many, a remembered unanswered prayer is reason enough to dismiss all future praying and sometimes even to doubt the possibility of communicating with the Divine. And it seems a fair enough question to ask, "What is the incentive for staying in conversation with a Divine who doesn't seem to respond to what you have to say?" If you pray these prayers to a Holy Other who you have been told loves you, wants to help you, and cares for you—and then your prayers are not answered, what are you to think?

## THE GIFT OF A NEW QUESTION

Sometimes what we need is the gift of a new question.

Perhaps the question—"Why are my prayers not answered?" or "Why should I keep on praying when I don't get what I pray for?"—can be replaced with an inquiry that is much more powerful.

We might ask questions like, "Why do I pray?" or "What is happening when I pray?" or "In how many different ways might my prayers be answered?" or "What is the value and purpose of praying even if I don't get a specific outcome?" This takes our act of communicating with the Divine out of what a friend of mine refers to, tongue-in-cheek, as a cash business and puts it into the arena of ongoing research.

## PRAYER AS ONGOING RESEARCH

God is always a surprise, if anything, Martin Luther once said. Prayer that is thought of as ongoing research is always going to be full of surprises—and full of mystery. (The Greek root for the word "mystery" means to shut one's mouth, to be struck speechless.) If we think of our conversing with the Divine as ongoing research, then Simone Weil's definition of prayer seems very fitting: "Prayer," she says, is "attention, turning aside to see." And there are a myriad of things about prayer to see.

## SOMETIMES WE GET WHAT WE PRAY FOR

Sometimes what we see is an answer to prayer that looks like a one-to-one-correspondence. A mother prays for her baby's fever to break and, in a matters of minutes, the child's temperature is normal. A small prayer group in Wichita, Kansas, prays over a three-year period for a decrease in crime in Wichita. At the end of the three years, the Chief of Police, who knows nothing about the prayer experiment, announces that crime has fallen by thirty-three percent in the city over the past three years, although no one can pinpoint why.

Once I was having difficulty while writing a book. I told my mother when we met for lunch that I could not get a certain chapter done. I went back to work that afternoon; and, suddenly, without explanation, around three o'clock, I felt enthusiasm return and clear direction for the chapter emerge. When I talked to my mother that night, she asked, "How did your writing go this afternoon?" I told her that the chapter was done and that I was happy with it. She replied, "Well, I started praying for you right after lunch. About middle of the afternoon, my intuition told me that the prayer had been answered, so I stopped praying and started cooking supper."

Coincidences all, some would say. But I'm reminded of the Englishman William Temple's assertion: "When I pray, coincidences happen, and when I do not, they don't."

## SOMETIMES WE GET POSITIVE EVIDENCE

In the late nineties, a researcher counted more than two hundred and fifty empirical studies that statistically prove the benefits of prayer. And this number, reported in epidemiological and medical literature since the 1800s, continues to grow. Many of us read or heard about one such study: 393 heart patients who were admitted to the coronary care unit at San Francisco General Hospital over a ten-month period who were included in an experiment involving prayer. Each of 192 patients among the 393 were prayed for daily by five to seven people who did not know the patients. The people who did the praying were given only the first names of the patients and their general conditions; they were not told what specifically to pray for. Doctors, nurses, and patients knew nothing about the experiment.

The scientific findings? Those prayed for were five times less likely to require antibiotics and three times less likely to develop cardiopulmonary arrest. None of the prayed-for patients required artificial respiration, while twelve of the other patients did. Fewer of them died than in the group not prayed for. "If the technique being studied had been a new drug or a surgical procedure instead of prayer," said Larry Dossey, M.D., "it would almost certainly have been heralded as some sort of breakthrough."

## SOMETIMES WE ARE HAPPY
## OUR PRAYERS WERE NOT ANSWERED

Sometimes what we see when we give attention is our good fortune that an earlier prayer was not answered. Garth Brooks, the country and western singer, sold millions of copies of a song in which a man runs into his old high school girlfriend years after she jilted him and broke his heart. Upon meeting her again, the guy can only say in deep gratitude, "Thank God for unanswered prayer." Each of us has some situation or event that, in hindsight, we are glad turned out some way other than the way we prayed.

## SOMETIMES THE ANSWER OCCURS OVER TIME

Sometimes what we see is gradual, almost imperceptible change. I remember when I began to pray several years ago about my temper. I was embarrassed at outbursts of anger that were beyond anything a particular circumstance called for. For a week, in my daily quiet time, I used the opening part of my spiritual practice to write about anger, to read verses from the Bible about anger, and to reflect on recent occurrences of my anger. Then I sat in silence. Afterward I prayed for release from this unpredictable, inappropriate anger. In a while I forgot I had prayed these prayers, but over time both my husband and I saw a change. I have no idea what happened, and I have no idea when it happened. I do know today I am free from those bouts of destructive anger.

## SOMETIMES THE ANSWER
## IS THAT WE ARE SUSTAINED

Ann and Barry Ulanov—Ann is an Episcopal priest and a Jungian analyst and Barry is an English professor—write about the many ways our prayers are answered. They say one of the main results we get from praying is we are kept from becoming totally exhausted in living our lives. In fact, they suggest that being able to rely on the Divine who is so much more powerful and creative than we are is prayer's identifying mark of protection. Prayer protects us from our pretensions to omnipotence and our inflated conviction that we can do it all, by connecting us to a larger Source that really can do everything.

## SOMETIMES THE ANSWER IS A SURPRISE

Sometimes what we see is an answer we would not have imagined. "Some deep and wise reordering of our little being opens us to the largeness of being in new ways," the Ulanovs tell us. We see a new direction. We feel connected in a way we hadn't felt connected before. We experience an enlivening of our Self—we feel more alive and real and more our own self. We get new ideas. We bump into someone whose presence enlarges us. We feel energy again.

## SOMETIMES THE ANSWER IS NEW POSSIBILITIES

An answer to one of our prayers might be a new way to feel and think and act about a specific situation or person, and we see this fresh vision is connected to our praying. Our sense of causality changes. "No longer does A inevitably lead straight to B. Now A opens into H and Q and M and P, as well as pointing to B. The straight line becomes curved, parabolic, inclusive. It is open to more than one possibility." When this happens, we start to live our lives in a rearranged form.

## SOMETIMES THE ANSWER
## COMES THROUGH ORDINARY HAPPENINGS

Sometimes the answers to our prayers come through events, little events in our own history. Little personal things that make connections that we could never prove rest on our prayer interventions but which make all the difference to us as we live the events. After living in a city for several months without finding the new friends that I had expected would appear quickly, I finally spent much of my prayer time one day lamenting about this situation. Shortly thereafter an old friend who had moved to town gave a dinner party to which I was invited. All five of the guests who came that night were women I liked immediately and whom I now see on a regular basis. An ordinary happening . . . an answer to prayer.

## SOMETIMES THE ANSWER
## IS AN INCREASE IN OUR CAPACITY TO SUFFER

The Old English meaning of the verb "to suffer" is to allow yourself to be subjected to something that is painful. Sometimes there is absolutely nothing that can be done about a situation except to make an assertion: I will feel this pain, I will acknowledge this pain, I will live through this pain. Through this experience, we become stronger. Our capacity to bear suffering increases. We are able to accept, without resentment, that suffering as an indelible part of our lives and the lives of others. This acceptance and the accompanying increased capacity to bear the suffering, ironically enough, we experience as an answer to our prayer.

## SOMETIMES THE ANSWER
## IS THAT WE LEARN BETTER HOW TO PRAY

Sometimes what we see about the answers to our prayers is that by praying we learn better how to pray. We learn to say, with Anthony Bloom, however well we pray, we are aware at every moment that our best idea may be wrong. Instead of asking for a particular thing for people we love, we may choose to ask instead for Divine presence to surround them, for these persons to flourish inwardly as God's goodness permeates all parts of their lives.

Howard Thurman tells a wonderful story about a ninety-year-old woman teaching him how to pray about specific people and situations. The woman was a member of a small New England church that was having an extended crisis with the minister. Here is how the woman told Dr. Thurman she prayed about the situation:

> *I gave myself plenty of time. I went into a thorough review of the highlights of the sixty years I have been a member of the church right up to the present situation. I talked it through very carefully. It was so good to talk freely and to know that the feelings and the thoughts behind the words were being understood. When I finished, I said, "Now, Father, these are the facts as best I can state them. Take them and do the best you can. I have no suggestions to make."*

I read this story several years ago, and I have tried (with more and less success, I have to say) to pray like this woman prayed:

- to state the facts as I see them in my conversation with the Divine,
- to try to make no suggestions about what ought to be done, and then,
- to leave the outcome to God.

## SOMETIMES THE ANSWER IS OUR OWN PERSISTENCE

The other side of this coin is the prayer of persistence where the person will not stop asking the Divine for a particular outcome. There is an old story about Abba Moses at Scetis who went on a journey to Petra. He worried as he traveled, wondering where he would find water when he got to his destination. A voice said to Abba Moses, "Go, and do not be anxious about anything." So he went.

Some Fathers came to see him in Petra, and by now Abba Moses had only a small bottle of water. He used all the water to cook lentils for his guests. Then he began to go in and out of his cell, praying until a cloud of rain came and filled all the cisterns.

The visitors asked him later why he had gone in and out of the cell so much. The Abba answered, "I was arguing with God, saying, 'You brought me here and now I have no water for your servants.' This is why I was going in and out; I was going on at God till God sent us some water."

I suppose the wisdom here is to know the difference—when, in all humility, to recognize that my ideas of what ought to happen, at their best, are limited and when to persist in praying for a particular thing to be done. There is no right answer. We have to grapple with the incongruities. Each of us prays in the way that is best for us. And that way may change as frequently as does the subject of our prayers.

## SOMETIMES THE ANSWER IS A CHANGE IN FOCUS

Sometimes what we see in our prayers is that, instead of thinking of God as a power we keep in store for our last push, we now think of the Divine as a Holy Other with whom to build an ongoing relationship. We see our prayers as an attempt to realize the love that unites us with everyone. We see our praying as a commitment to allow this love to be more present to us and to give this love greater scope to act on us. In the building of this Divine and human relationship, we find doubt not so much answered as lived through. What we concentrate on is not realizing specific outcomes to our praying but uncovering more and more of our Self, our own being, by communing with ultimate Being, God.

## SOMETIMES WE SEE THAT THE VERY ACT OF PRAYING IS THE ANSWER

One thing we do definitely see over time is that praying benefits us. Even if we do not get our requests, it does us good to pray. Prayer is a back and forth movement between us and the Divine that will go on for the rest of our lives. Prayer is the link between your new self that is in constant transformation into the image of love, the image of God, and your old self with whom you must come to terms if you are to be transformed. The prayers you pray in your daily spiritual practice are—no matter the outcome—an encounter with the Divine. Your praying is a shared life with God. As the anonymous writer of *The Cloud of Unknowing* says, let prayer deal with us and lead us wherever it would like. "Meddle not with it . . . be the tree and let it be the carpenter. Be the house and let it be the householder dwelling inside."

So the important thing comes to be the act of praying, not the outcome. The point is not to know when, how, or where a particular prayer will be answered but to find the strength, the direction, and the depth within yourself that come when you deliberately and consciously connect and grow in intimacy with the Divine. Every time you pray you get at least four things: Divine Presence (which is always there when we pray, regardless of whether we feel anything or not); strength (that is extra, beyond our customary day-in, day-out capabilities); counsel (a quiet guidance, a knowing, a turn to a particular direction that may happen imperceptibly over time); and contact (with love, which is all and the core of who we are). No wonder, then, that millions and millions of people around the globe every day respond like the Psalmist of Israel: "My heart has heard you say, 'Come and talk with me,' And my heart responds, 'Lord, I am coming.'"

Prayer has sustained human beings as far back as we have written record. Prayer is a call from the heart to One who both lives in and holds our heart. Prayer makes the actions and attitudes of our best self more and more available in daily life because prayer aligns us with the Good. Prayer changes us. And, by changing us, prayer then changes the world.

## R E F L E C T I O N

*What do you expect when you pray?*

## SACRED TASK

The Puritan in me always chided: if you were a better person, if you did more, if you behaved a certain way, God would be more likely to answer your prayers. I see now that I thought this way because I not only expected the exact answer to my prayer, but I expected it immediately. When I internalized that I was praying for the long haul and praying for more awareness of my constant connection with the Divine, no matter how the specifics of my current situations turned out, I stopped checking up to see how well I was praying. This was a turning point in my spiritual life.

TASK: Consider any unexamined assumptions you have about successful prayer. Have you experienced any events or experiences that included prayers which were not answered as someone desired? What effect did this have on the person praying? On those who knew about the prayers? What do you expect now when you pray?

I found out many years ago that my connection to God is paramount in my life. After years of success in the business world, I woke up in my early forties and realized that I was not happy. My wife and I had a good life; the kids were out on their own; but I felt restless, empty, and discontent. I describe it as a holy unrest.

I changed careers, taking a job that focused totally on serving others. In the eighteen years since, I've become clear what my priorities are: God, family, work. My goal now is to know God, not know about God. I've learned that the only way I can know God is to set aside enough time for this to happen.

I am an early riser, usually at 5 A.M. This gives me plenty of time to "waste" with God and to do what I need to do to get ready for the day. I generally read Scripture first and then reflect on what I've just read. I also use the twenty-minute drive to work to do my praying.

My anxiety about the ups and downs of life has decreased enormously as a result of this daily spiritual discipline. The way I think about this is probably an oversimplification, but there is an element of truth in it: Every event and situation in life is no more nor less than an equipping process for the next step, until we take the final step. The sooner I am able to accept this truth in each challenging circumstance, the more I am able to adjust to the roller coaster of living. My experience is that nothing is wasted in God's economy.

—E. S., businessman, manager

*Part Four*

*Chapter Ten*

⚜

# LIVING AN ALIGNED LIFE

*We and God have business with each other.*

—*William James*

Over the years, I have seen that this practice of daily quiet time and prayer is not the purview of just certain people who have religious callings. I know scientists, mothers of preschoolers, attorneys, gardeners, secretaries, business executives, carpenters, law enforcement personnel, consultants, managers, plumbers, dancers . . . all of whom have a consistent spiritual practice of quiet time and prayer. These people are from many age groups and from many different backgrounds and cultures.

What calls such a diverse group of individuals to a spiritual practice? When I ask, they cite many reasons:

*Life getting more and more hectic and disjointed and wanting to do something to change it; Having an intense desire for calm, peace, and hope; Knowing someone who is committed to a spiritual practice and seeing in that person's life something inspiring; Having a desire to pray; Experiencing some tragic event that made it clear that an individual is ultimately not in control; Knowing there must be more to living than they are experiencing; Wanting to find more purpose and meaning in what they do every day; Feeling empty.*

Way back in the sixth century, Augustine, the great thinker, philosopher, and spiritual writer, spoke for all of us who first seek outside for what will bring meaning and peace and, only after that pales or disappoints, turn to honor our rich inner life: "For thee were we made, O God, and our hearts are restless until they find their rest in thee." Until that fit is found, until our hearts settle into their true home, we do look but not find, gather but not enjoy, try but not relish the fruits of our trying.

I remember being startled—literally jerking my head up and sitting back in my chair—the day I chanced upon a statement by an ancient spiritual master, Theophan the Recluse. This is what he said that hit me so strongly: "Most people are like a shaving of wood which is curled round its central emptiness."

At the time no words could have described my life more accurately. I had achieved what seemed to me an extraordinary amount of success for someone from my circumstances: a full professorship by age thirty-nine, a book that contributed to a positive and major change of direction in my academic discipline, a lovely home, a luxury sports car, the opportunity to travel. But I still felt like a shaving of wood curled round its own emptiness. Everything was external. Everything was measured against some standard or expectation or high bar set by someone else, somebody out there. My life was not my own. I was not in touch with my own being.

But the good news was that the urge to connect was still present in my heart. The desire to have life mean something was still strong. The recognition that something important was not being paid attention to was clear. An Indian sage said once that we all feel a nudge from the Divine every twenty-four hours. I don't know about the every twenty-four hours part of that assertion, but I do know about the nudge. It was there.

I've thought about this a lot. What does keep drawing us to a higher aim? What pulls us to know and be our true Self? What is there about how we are made that won't let us feel whole and complete until we are in touch with Holy Being? What is there about aligning with the Divine—and, hence, with the best part of ourselves—that makes us feel more centered and balanced?

Thomas Merton said it like this: Each of us is an individual image of God. Just as God is the free and creative Source of love for and to us, we are a free and creative source of a gift of love and meaning to ourselves and to others. If this gift that we are is not made and given, Merton says, it is irreplaceable and cannot be given by anybody else.

Huston Smith, a spiritual thinker and writer now in his later years, said something very similar when he spoke recently at a gathering near where I live:

> *If we do not become our Self, there is a hole left in the big, sweeping net of life where we should have been. No other individual—no matter how famous, enlightened, whatever they may be . . . past, present, or future—can fill the hole that is ours, just as we cannot fill the one that is theirs. It is our assignment and ours alone. That is how important who we are, what we do here, who we become is.*

It is my experience there is no better support for carrying out this assignment, to become able to give and receive love fully, than our daily spiritual practice.

The age-old commandment sums up the main mission of our lives: "Thou shalt love the Lord, thy God, with all thy

heart, soul, and strength and thy neighbor as thyself." This is the
secret of everything. God's image—love—remains in us, often
covered over but always still there. Every day we include a spiritual practice in our schedule we uncover—and recover—a bit
more love.

## NOT EASY BUT NATURAL

I grew up hearing an old saying used to describe an activity that
would require no effort to accomplish: it is as easy as falling off
a log. I've tried walking across enough logs over creeks and
streams while hiking in the Smoky Mountains to know that it
does take nothing to slip! I won't begin to assert that keeping a
spiritual discipline is as easy as falling off a log, because it isn't.
But I will say that the connection, the imprint, the pull and
desire to connect with the Divine is as easy as falling off a log
because it is part of who we are. This connection is natural.

Look at the act of praying.

People pray all over the world. People pray in all kinds of
cultures. People pray about all kinds of things and in all kinds of
circumstances. People pray at all ages.

Here is a prayer I heard when I traveled in Africa a few
years ago:

*Lord, the motor under me is running hot.*
*Lord, there are twenty-eight people and lots of luggage in*
    *this truck.*
*Underneath are my bad tires.*
*The brakes are unreliable.*
*Unfortunately I have no money, and parts are difficult to get. . . .*
*Lord, I trust you!*
*Passing large churches in every village, I am reminded of you,*

*And in reverence I take off my hat.*
*Now downhill in second gear.*

—*Prayer from Ghana, West Africa*

This prayer one of my Irish friends taught me:

*God, let those that love us, love us;*
*And those that don't love us*
*May You turn their hearts;*
*And if You don't turn their hearts*
*May You turn their ankles*
*So we'll know them by their limping.*

—*Irish Prayer*

Here is a beautifully simple prayer I've heard friends from India pray:

*Wonderful, wonderful, wonderful.*

—*Ancient Hindu prayer*

This prayer my brother Frank heard from Ashley, his five-year-old, as he put her to bed the night before her grandmother's funeral:

*Jesus, bless Grandmother up in heaven, and help her take care of God.*

—*A prayer of a child*

Human beings everywhere display this tendency to call out to a Holy Other. The communication may be as automatic as "Oh, my God," when bad news comes or "Thank God" when disaster is averted. It may be as conscious and directed as the gentle request, "Grant me, O God, the heart of a child, pure and transparent as a spring day. . . ." Or as calm as the words of gratitude, "Having passed over this day, Lord, I give thanks unto

thee. The evening draweth nigh, make it comfortable . . . "
Whether spontaneous or deliberate, we human beings talk to a
Presence that is other than ourselves.

The very act of our praying makes a bold assertion: there
exists some One, some Spirit, some Force, some Power that is
Other than us and this Other has abilities, knowledge, awareness,
energy, and powers we do not have. Praying, whether spontaneous or planned, supposes this Holy Other will listen to us and
respond in some way to our communication. Praying supposes,
in some inexplicable fashion, we human beings and this *Spiritus
Creator* are intimately related.

When you think about it, it's amazing. That, innately, human
beings in cultures around the world know they are connected to
the very fountainhead of life, to the creator of everything. And
they know they can rightfully think of this relationship as a
source of help, care, friendship, and healing love. People everywhere know God accompanies them in the darkest of places and
dances with them when the day turns light.

What a resource. What a companion. What an attending power.

## BUT WE FORGET

Martin Buber once wrote this stirring affirmation: "That you
need God more than anything, you know at all times in your
heart. . . . You need God in order to be. . . ." You'd think we'd
remember this every second of every day. You'd think that, in this
astonishing intimate relationship of friendship and love, we'd
consciously and confidently lean back in the knowledge that
peace and wisdom, sustaining power and quiet were just as close
as the breath we breathe.

But life happens.

And we so quickly forget.

Over and over we have to be reminded and to remind our-selves that this astounding connection, this relationship, between us and the Divine exists. While experiencing the connection is as easy as falling off a log, remembering to pay attention to the connection isn't.

## THE VALUE OF OUR SPIRITUAL DISCIPLINE

A thousand times a day we are faced with the choice of respond-ing from our best selves or from some other part of our make-up. If you are like me, the ratio of best-self choices to other-self choices is often low. What people have discovered over time, however, is that as they carry out their spiritual practice, that ratio improves. For in a daily spiritual practice we are visiting this place where love and our best Self reside.

What are you accessing when you bring yourself to quiet, listen in silence, and pray in spoken words?

I hear many different responses:

*There's an access to quiet and calm . . . to my own truth, voice, and wisdom . . . to an experience of being loved deeply, beyond words . . . to unexpected thoughts that turn out to help solve some of my most vexing problems . . . to surprises and to beau-tiful gifts of moments of pure grace . . . to a natural movement in my life toward what gives me purpose and meaning . . . to being myself . . . to finding a true center from which to move out and live my busy life . . . to peace even when my external life is in turmoil . . . to a kind of gentle guidance that takes me to people and places I would not have gone before . . . to a sense of wholeness . . . to the recognition that I have an intimate rela-tionship with God that will always be present, no matter what happens . . . to a new strength that I find quite amazing. . . .*

## YOUR ROLE IN THE MATTER

We have all read the sad accounts. A baby shrivels, physically and emotionally, from the absence of human touch. A family disintegrates because no one remembered to do the work it takes to communicate. A friendship dwindles simply because no one noticed the drifting apart.

Relationships don't just flourish on their own. Connections don't automatically stay live and active. I remember a conversation once at a restaurant when my best friend and I joined a few others for supper. One man at the table remarked at one point in the evening about the strength of Rita's and my friendship. "It takes a lot of work," Rita answered. "The only thing I give more attention to than this friendship is my marriage."

Our relationship with God, too, requires attention in order to flourish. It's not that it disappears if we don't pay attention. The connection is always there. But to develop that connection is often the harder path. In one of those movies I can watch again and again—and do—Bill Murray plays the role of a young man searching for what will give his life meaning. He finally meets a holy man who tells him he must go back out into life and maintain his experience of things sacred even as he conducts his daily affairs. "It is like walking the razor's edge," the holy man tells him, using the words that are also the name of the movie.

No question that for you and me, as easy as falling off the log, it isn't. But even someone as unskilled as I am finally learned to walk the log over a rushing stream, by giving focus and attention. The rewards are worth every bit of the effort. And the losses are too significant to overlook.

If we don't give time and pay attention, we don't thrive in the way we are meant to. We don't grow in the kind of wisdom that comes from communicating with the Divine. We live beneath our possibility; we fail to recognize our fullest purpose. We don't settle into the natural fit between God and us. Somehow things always seem a little out of sync. We don't find home.

Keeping our spiritual practice of quiet time and prayer is a way we remember. A way we remember consistently and intentionally that *Spiritus Creator* is the free and creative source of everything we love, everything that gives us meaning. A way we recall that we are created for and called to love. A way we ask for help; the way we offer thanks. A way we give; the way we receive. A way we love others, love God, love ourselves.

## R E F L E C T I O N

*Think back to Theophan's words: Most people are like a shaving of wood curled round its central emptiness. Is there any relationship of these words to your life? What do you see people (or yourself) doing to attempt to fill a central emptiness?*

### SACRED TASK

Thinking about the assertion by the sage from India that each of us receives a nudge from the Divine every twenty-four hours, I wonder in how many ways that nudge might come: reaching for the hand of a child, feeling genuine concern for the street person into whose cup we drop a dollar, praying for someone we know who is in trouble, rubbing our elderly parent's back, deciding spontaneously to dart into a church on the corner to sit in the quiet for a few minutes.

TASK: Think back on the past twenty-four hours to see if you can identify a nudge you received from the Divine.

Although I'm sure the correct thing to do is close your eyes, get still, breathe deeply, and enter a meditative state, I find I need something to connect to. The best are things that connect me to my childhood. The water sounds of the hill country where I grew up are now replicated in the waterfalls we built at our new home. I even brought in rocks from the hill country. These sounds of water connect me to the Source.

Early in our marriage, we lived with very meager means; and I still found it possible to connect to the Source in unexpected ways. A packet of seeds could give me a real connection to Mother Earth. Once I built an altar out of hay in a barn. The roots of an old tree down by the creek were my seat in a cathedral.

Books, too, have been a huge part of the spiritual life of our family, and I find great inspiration in my library. Keeping the books clear in my line of vision, I turn my chair to face the east—I just purchased a very wonderful, comfortable chair—and I sit still right there for hours. I shut the library doors, sometimes turn on music, sometimes not. I look out at the antique roses in our front yard and watch the seasons change.

—M. M. W., novelist

✿

## Chapter Eleven

# SURVIVING THE WINDSTORMS

*Love's direction guards us not against*
*grief but against a darkening of the heart.*
—John Dunne

There's a wonderful story of St. Teresa of Avila talking back one day to God. It seems that the abbess was very ill, in bed, with the flu. The weather was stormy and cold. Sometime during the day she heard God's voice tell her to get up from her sickbed and have someone hitch her horse to its cart. She was needed some distance away to do the work of the Lord.

The good sister dragged herself out of bed and got dressed to go across the countryside in the terrible weather. As she progressed along her journey, the horse stumbled on a bridge that spanned a fast-rushing stream. The cart slipped and ended up hanging off the side of the narrow wooden bridge, with St. Teresa holding onto the side of the cart. The cold rain hit her full force as the high winds whipped. She looked up and said to God, "My dear Lord, is this the way you treat your friends?" When she heard God answer, "Yes, my child, it is," St. Teresa responded, "Well, it is no wonder that you have so few of them."

## WHEN LIFE IS UNFAIR

All of us have felt this way at some time. Life has been unfair. We have borne the brunt of something we did not deserve to suffer. Loss has surprised and diminished us. Hard work has not paid off. A dream has turned to smoke. Good fortune has turned to bad. Tragedy has hit in a seemingly random pattern.

Or sometimes even worse . . . nothing. You feel blank. Empty. Dry. Listless. Off center and you don't know why. You feel unable to care about much of anything. No enthusiasm, no energy. Standing perilously on the brink of an abyss.

How can such things be, when you are working hard to keep a daily spiritual practice? Is this any kind of reward for a commitment to connecting with the source of all calm and love? Where is the promised peace and balance of daily quiet time and prayer to be found when you are buffeted by the windstorms of life?

## SPARROW CAUGHT BY THE CAT'S CLAW

In my experience, this contradiction is one of the hardest issues to unknot. If I am trying to be as good a person as I can be, committed to doing my part in an ongoing dialogue with the Holy Other, why do terrible things still happen in my life? Why do I find myself at times feeling so out of touch, so alone, so empty? Why am I and the ones I love not better shielded and protected? These seem legitimate questions to ask. If the same things happen to people who dedicate themselves to spiritual growth as happen to people who make no attempt to connect with the Divine, what's the difference? What's the use?

If it's any consolation, many people over the ages have wrestled with such questions. Two of the brightest minds to think about the relationship of the Divine to human beings trying to make it in a topsy-turvy world were the women theologians from the twelfth and thirteenth centuries, Hildegard of Bingen and Dame Julian of Norwich. Julian, buffeted with a painful illness that lasted for several years, found this equilibrium:

*God did not say:*
*You will not be tempested.*
*You will not labor hard.*
*You will not be troubled.*
*But God did say:*
*You will not be overcome.*

Julian also wrote,

*Just so the wonder is not that people suffer, for the world holds pain and sorrow enough for all of us. Neither need we wonder why God does not put things right again, for God is already at work on the great deed. God is already beginning to make all things well. No, the wonder is that people who have been broken like sparrows caught by a cat's claw should find three strengths: the strength to go on living, the strength to continue their search for God, and the strength to reach out to others, to give and receive compassion.*

"Broken like sparrows caught by a cat's claw." Do we ever know what the lady means! I felt that way when my grandfather committed suicide. When my husband, Greg, dropped dead. When I changed careers voluntarily only to find myself without money or clear direction. When, two years ago, my parents died unexpectedly, eight days apart. When last year's good fortune brought my husband a wonderful new job opportunity but required us to leave people and a place we dearly loved. You, too, I know, have your own caught-in-the-cat's-claw experiences.

But what about the strengths Julian asserts we do find, in spite of our pain? The strength to go on living, the strength to continue our search for God, the strength to reach out to others. Are these strengths real, or was she just a-dreaming?

I saw someone just this morning who ought to know. A couple of years ago my acquaintance, a very successful entrepreneur in a major American city, found out she had breast cancer. Wham. Whop. Broken like a sparrow caught by a cat's claw. An operation followed. Chemotherapy. Loss of her beautiful hair. Sick as a dog for days at a time. Then a long, slow recovery.

Today we sat on the deck of my home and talked about how our lives had changed. Tears came to her eyes as she told me how central her spiritual life has become in all she does. She has sold her businesses. She lives on a farm in a quiet place. Her occupation is now photography; and a current project is a collection of which she hopes will become a book, beautiful photographs of women who have had cancer.

Julian's three strengths: "the strength to go on living, the strength to continue the search for God, and the strength to reach out to others, to give and to receive compassion." Yes, my friend is a living testimony to the emergence of these strengths that came during the worst windstorms of her life.

### WITHERED STICKS AND SOULS TURNED GREEN
It is easy to see, reading Hildegard of Bingen, why, of all the times we would want to stay in touch with the Divine, the most important is on those hard, cold, empty, angry, confusing, dry days when most everything seems senseless:

> *The Spirit is Life, movement, color, radiance, restorative*
>     *stillness in the din.*
> *The Spirit's power makes all withered sticks and souls green*
>     *again with the juice of life.*

*The Spirit plays music in the soul . . . gathers the perplexed,*
*strengthens and heals.*
*The Spirit awakens mighty hope, blowing everywhere the*
*winds of renewal in creation.*
*And this is the Mystery of God in whom we live and move*
*and have our being.*

Each of us has experienced ourselves or someone else growing green again with the juice of life after feeling far too long like
a withered stick. When, many years ago, my husband, in perfect
health, dropped dead while jogging, I was frightened, lost, with no
sense that life could ever be good again. Things that I loved before
were now meaningless. The beautiful red and lime and indigo and
violet yarns that always enticed me to the loom in my weaving
room were now invisible to my eyes. The sounds of the symphony—or even my favorite country/western singers—were like
tin in my ears. Food felt like sand in my mouth.

Then one day, while I was standing at the kitchen sink, an
image flashed in front of my eyes: the forsythia bush that had
grown outside my bedroom window when I was a young girl.
Its long fronds were that color of new spring green that looks lit
from the inside and were covered with hundreds and hundreds
of bright yellow flowers. In the moment of seeing that image, I
felt a ray of hope.

Today I know this truth: grief, when it is fully experienced,
can be integrated and life can again be biding, full, and new. An
image I often conjure up to represent my life—birth to now—
is a mosaic like those brightly colored mosaics laid in the floors
and porticos of Roman houses in ancient times. The mosaics
made a big picture—perhaps in this section a woman carrying a
jug on her head; in that, a man with one foot hoisted on his
chariot; in another, children playing with a toy.

I think now of that awful experience of Greg's death and the dark, empty time of my grieving as a black section in my mosaic— maybe a heavy stormy sky or a place deep in a forest where light has a hard time getting through. But around that black place in my mosaic are many other scenes, of all different shapes and hues. The picture wouldn't be complete without the black sections, but neither is the mosaic only the dark sections. I step back and see the whole of my life—scenes bright, dark, predictable, surprising, old, new—and honor every part of the picture because each part has made me who I am today.

And that who I am today is a woman eager to live life fully. I remarried some years ago; and Jerele, my husband, did a beautiful thing when he asked me to marry him. The first toast of champagne—after I said yes so fast I think it surprised him—was to us and our future. Then Jerele proposed a second toast: to my late husband, though Jerele had never known him. With glasses clinking, we drank to the indestructibility of the power of love.

## A GOOD PAIR OF BOOTS AND THE THORNS

When we keep our daily spiritual practice active, during the bad times as well as the good, we are putting ourselves in the way of the Spirit that Hildegard describes, the Spirit of Life that renews, that resurrects, that turns death into life. We are focusing on strengthening our interior life, no matter the external circumstances surrounding us.

There's a Buddhist lesson that teaches the value of doing our inner work instead of trying to change all the unpleasant things around us. The story goes like this:

*If you're in a country where there are many thorns, and you set out to destroy the thorns, thinking the problem is the thorns, you will never be finished. But if you put on a good strong pair of boots and chaps, you can go where you like and the thorns will not harm you. It is really quite a bit easier to put on a good pair of shoes than to cover the earth trying to eradicate all the thorns.*

Doing our spiritual discipline, day in and day out, no matter what is going on in our inner and outer worlds, helps us, in the words of the Buddhist story, fashion the shoes of tolerance, enlightenment, and patience. Then we can go—in those shoes— into the tough brambles. We can deal with our problems, aid others, even help them make their own shoes. But if you just rush out to try to eradicate the brambles, you end up being shot full of thorns, paralyzed, ruined, and unable to benefit anybody else. How, in the face of truths like these, can we afford not to practice our spiritual discipline, even when the times are hard?

## LIVING TO THE OTHER SIDE OF THE HARD TIMES

The words Michael Horvit wrote on a basement wall in Cologne, Germany, during the Holocaust have been set to beautiful liturgical music:

*I believe in the sun even when it is not shining.*
*I believe in love even when feeling it not.*
*I believe in God even when God is silent.*

And Elie Wiesel, the Nobel prize-winning writer, speaks to the presence of the Divine even in and through the darkest times. He wrote a letter to God, printed in the *New York Times*, some fifty years after being held prisoner in a concentration camp:

*What about my faith in you, Master of the Universe? I now realize I never lost it, not even over there, during the darkest hours of my life. I don't know why I kept on whispering my daily prayers and the ones reserved for the Sabbath, and for the holidays, but I did recite them, often with my father and, on Rosh ha Shanah eve, with hundreds of inmates of Auschwitz. . . . But my faith was no longer pure. How could it be? It was filled with anguish rather than fervor, with perplexity more than piety. . . .*

*At one point, I began wondering whether I was not unfair with you. After all, Auschwitz was not something that came down ready-made from heaven. It was conceived by men, implemented by men, staffed by men. And their aim was to destroy not only us but you as well. Ought we not to think of your pain, too? Watching your children suffer at the hands of your other children, haven't you also suffered?*

This is a deep mystery, how in the depths of suffering, hope against hope is born. Through our connection with God we are given not necessarily power-over but we are given power-with, the power to be with the pains and sufferings that are part of all our lives. This power-with is the shape of love against the very forces of death and non-being.

Even when we are driven to the depths of defeat and despair, we can and do experience, in the words of theology writer Peter Hodgson, the "miraculous ability to start over, to build afresh, to maintain a struggle and a vision. A future is opened up through even the most negative experience . . . the victory arrives through the living communion of love." We do come out on the other side of the windstorms of life.

## REFLECTION

*If having a daily spiritual practice is not insurance against loss and pain, what does it provide that wards off our becoming bitter and like a withered stick?*

## SACRED TASK

Rabbi Marc Gellman and Father Tom Hartman, the sprightly voices of "The God Squad" who write magazine columns and books on theological issues, assert that God allows humans to make a difference in their own and others' lives. "Life is a journey," they say, "in which we learn how to take care of ourselves, help others and turn bad things to our advantage."

Rabbi Gellman says God could eliminate evil but such an action would eliminate the free will that causes evil. "If you're forced to do good because God says so," he explains, "it is impossible to love God or serve God freely." And moral wrongs are "a direct consequence of free will. God has no involvement: Humans make their own choices and act on animal impulses."

When natural disasters like earthquakes, tornadoes, fires, and floods occur, the Rabbi and Father go on to say, people suffer, but that doesn't mean God has abandoned them. Rather, we are empowered to protect and help ourselves and others when such disaster strikes. We also have the ability to use turmoil and even tragedy to find goodness in our lives—"be it in the form of natural beauty, good deeds done, or lessons learned from parents, friends, and elders. Goodness occurs every day, but you need to train your eyes to see it. What seems limiting can really be an opportunity to do good."

TASK: Do you know persons whose actions and lives corroborate what Rabbi Gellman and Father Hartman assert? Someone who has used turmoil and even tragedy to find goodness in their lives? Someone who learned how to turn bad things to advantage? To help others?

I have wanted to do quiet time for as long as I remember. For me, it was always about a responsibility to read the Bible every day. I really tried. I bought every read-through-the-Bible-in-a-year book ever printed. But I could not keep it up. The whole practice seemed externally imposed rather than internally driven.

The shift came when I began to hear ideas about sitting quietly and letting God talk to you, how quiet time was really that—quiet time. I began to yearn for a time when I didn't have to do anything but sit and listen.

The transformation did not happen all at once. There were lots of starts and stops. But now this time is the most important part of my day. If I practice my quiet time, my day is better—not the circumstances, but I am better in the circumstances. If I don't practice quiet time, the day has me.

I often do silent prayer as I swim. During the twenty to thirty minutes it takes me to do my laps, I keep my eyes on the black lane line and repeat the words, "My mind is stayed on thee, O Lord." This is a very important silent and surrender time for me, a person of many words. (After all, one of the things I do for a living is write and speak!) It is a time of real meditation.

I finish the morning quiet time with an exercise of breathing out resentment, breathing in joy; breathing out anxiety, breathing in peace; breathing out want, breathing in thanksgiving; breathing out hate, breathing in love; breathing out worry, breathing in trust. Then I am ready to start my day.

—E. A. S., president,
 international communications consulting firm

## Chapter Twelve

༖

# CELEBRATING THE LONG
# VIEW

*Life is probably round.*
*—Vincent Van Gogh*

From silly devotions and from sour-faced saints, good Lord,
deliver us." This is a famous prayer of St. Teresa of Avila, and I have
always loved the invocation because it is a great reminder of perspective. We have seen enough long-faced folks to know this is not
who we ever want to become. We commit to daily sacred quiet
time and prayer not as a penance, not as an obligation, but as a joy-
ful expression of who we are, of our very being. We establish a spiritual practice because we know we cannot be genuinely content,
nor deeply satisfied, nor firmly anchored unless we experience a
connection and a relationship with the Holy Other. As Pascal, the
French scientist, said: "We all have a God-shaped vacuum in our
hearts, and we are not happy until that vacuum is filled."

## THE OUTCOME OF QUIET TIME AND PRAYER

What can we expect to be an outcome of having a daily spiritual practice? What will happen in our lives as days turn into

months and months turn into years and we continue to connect with God in a private, personal, and consistent way? One of my favorite stories about outcomes tells of a blacksmith in Kentucky who made a commitment to pray the ancient Eastern Orthodox *Jesus Prayer* every day as often as possible . . . "Lord, Jesus Christ, Son of God, have mercy on me, a sinner." "I'll give it twenty years," he said, "and if nothing comes of this practice in that amount of time, I'll just give it up." So he practiced the prayer as he rode in his truck from farm to farm, as he shoed horses, as he lay in his bed at night.

At the end of twenty years, the blacksmith spoke to an Orthodox priest who was visiting Kentucky. When the blacksmith told the priest that he practiced the *Jesus Prayer* daily, the priest asked him what had happened in his life as a result of all this praying. Did he, for instance, have any of the phantasmagorias that some people associate with the spiritual? "You mean the lights and colors and all that?" the blacksmith answered, "Oh, I might have seen some; but, you know, things like that are really not the point." "And you really did this practice for twenty years?" the priest inquired. "Yes," the blacksmith answered. "This is the twentieth year—and here we are."

What I like about this story is the blacksmith stopped long ago looking for results and outcomes. He wasn't after titillating experiences. He wasn't measuring the value of his prayers by some yardstick of loss or gain. He wasn't expecting a particular outcome. Meister Eckhard, though he was speaking in the thirteenth century, could be talking, in these words, about someone today: "Some people want to see God with their eyes as they see a cow and to love God as they love their cow—they love their cow for the milk and cheese and profit it makes them." But these words don't fit the blacksmith from Kentucky. His daily spiritual practice was just what it was. And from the sounds of things, the prayer was definitely a source of wisdom and calm. Here he was, where he was, how he was, as he completed his twentieth year.

## INTANGIBLE AND UNEXPECTED GIFTS
## AND SURPRISES

The more we practice quiet time and prayer the more we count the gifts and surprises and moments of grace as lagniappe— something extra given at no cost—and the more we treasure the day-in, day-out bedrock certainties and peace and serenity that come with honoring our inner lives by connecting to the source of our very existence.

Yet we feel gratitude for the answers to prayer, the sense of direction, the bolts of joy that do come out of our daily spiritual discipline. I remember once being very upset with someone who had announced she would no longer be part of a holiday tradition that had come to mean a lot to me and the other women in our study group. In the praying-with-words part of my quiet time, I asked for help in loving this person anyway, and I prayed for release from my upset. While nothing happened during the prayer time itself, some hours later, as I walked from the kitchen to the dining room of my home—the subject of my prayer far from my mind by this time—a thought struck me: This decision does not mean the same thing to her that it does to you. The truth of that simple sentence permeated my being in a split second. The anger dissipated. I knew this thought was an answer to my morning prayer.

There are times when guidance comes during the moments of quiet. Once, as I sat in silence during my daily spiritual disci- pline, I thought of a young woman who had been in my home only once. The image of this person, whom I knew only slightly, stayed in my mind after I finished my quiet time and prayer. I decided to call her. I did not know her number, but I knew someone who did know her and could give me the information I needed.

I got her number and dialed it. The telephone rang many times. Finally, the young woman answered. She was sobbing, almost in hysterics. Her husband had just that morning told her he was leaving her. I invited her to come to my house for a cup of tea as soon as we got off the phone, and she agreed. We had a visit that was the beginning of a relationship that is filled, for both of us today, with companionship and love. (In fact, she and her new husband told me recently, if the baby they are expecting is a girl, she will be my namesake.)

What happened during that period of quiet time?

I like how Dr. Elizabeth Johnson talks about such experiences:

> . . . *since the mystery of God undergirds the whole world . . . just plain ordinary human life can be grist for the mill of experience of Spirit . . . everywhere true life exists, there the Spirit of God is at work . . . the Spirit's saving presence in the conflictual world is recognized to be everywhere, somehow always drawing near and passing by, shaping fresh starts of vitality and freedom.*

Kierkegaard, the philosopher, said a long time ago, "Prayer involves becoming silent, and being silent, and waiting until God is heard." That morning as I sat in quiet and listened, God was heard.

## THE GREATEST VALUE

So there are at times clear and visible outcomes that accrue from a daily spiritual practice. Still, this is not the greatest value. The greatest value is much more subtle, much more undefined and indescribable. And of much greater significance. For, ultimately, you are not concerned with the kinds of outcomes that can be described in verifiable terms, such as "It rained yesterday," or "The rose bush this morning has a dozen new buds," or even "My anxiety disappeared." (Many times you never get a specific thing you pray for. Many times you experience only long spells of dryness.)

Your daily spiritual practice, instead, puts you in touch with the depths of your wholeness and with the integrity of your very Self. You find through quiet time and prayer you move— aiming to arrive yet always in process—toward the core of who you are and who you want to be, a person of love. As musician and professor John Dunne says, "By remembering love, by remembering God, then I begin to know myself, to know my heart." You chose to listen, and you chose to set out in the direction of love, "from and of and towards God, and of inner peace."

## YOUR PERSONAL SACRED STORY

To know ourselves, to know our heart, is to know that our daily spiritual practice does not make us perfect. I laugh, recognizing myself, every time I read the prayer:

> *Dear Lord,*
> *So far today, God, I have done it right.*
> *I haven't gossiped, haven't lost my temper,*
> *haven't been greedy, grumpy, nasty, selfish*
> *or over-indulgent.*
> *I'm very thankful for that.*
> *But in a few minutes, Lord,*
> *I'm going to have to get out of bed.*
> *And from then on,*
> *I'm probably going to need a lot more help.*

What you become as a result of your commitment to a daily spiritual practice is someone who over time grows to have more tolerance, more equanimity, more humility. And you come to be more and more a person who knows his or her inner strength, knows that what is internal is far more powerful than what is external, knows that your ability to give and receive love will continue, as a result of your quiet time and prayer, to expand for the rest of your life. And with this expansion of being able to give and receive love comes what we most desire: a certainty that neither death nor life . . . principalities nor powers . . . things present or things to come . . . shall separate me from the love of God.

Through the practice of your daily spiritual discipline you are continuing to write your personal sacred story. Your sacred story is an account of how you conceptualize and communicate your response to divine and human encounters. The future direction of your narrative, Dr. Verena Kast asserts, always is the arena for possibility. (Every good story answers the question, "What happens next?") Life is going somewhere. Our lives are going somewhere. Being means on the way, en route. Every day that you make a space for your Self, listen to the silence, and pray you are farther along on your journey.

Journey to what possibility? As you continue each day in practicing your spiritual discipline, you will gain confidence and hope of the most positive sort. You will come to recognize that one never knows when the Divine will break through, that the possibility for breaking through is present every moment. You will experience knowing you are always, no matter what the circumstance, being carried by Life. You will gain a trusting anticipation of the future based on your understanding of a God who is trustworthy and who calls each of us into an open-ended future.

This means as you cement—and celebrate—your ongoing relationship with the Divine you can respond to thoughts of tomorrow with lively expectation, even excitement. Security lies in your relationship with God, not in particular events. For God wants abundant life, justice, and mercy to be part of life in the present.

## ALWAYS MOVING, NEVER ARRIVING

This is a lifelong journey, nothing to be accomplished overnight. And we are always progressing, even when that progression seems only inches at a time. There is a story told by the Fathers and Mothers of the Desert whose communities thrived in the 600s in Egypt:

> *A man had a plot of land. And through his carelessness brambles sprang up and it became a wilderness of thistles and thorns. Then he decided to cultivate it. So he said to his son: "Go and clear that ground." So the son went to clear it, and saw that the thistles and thorns had multiplied. . . . He said: "How much time shall I need to clear and weed all this?" And he lay on the ground and went to sleep. He did this day after day. Later his father came to see what he had done, and found him doing nothing. When his father asked him about it, the son replied that the job looked so hard that he could never make himself begin. His father replied, "Son, if you had cleared each day the area on which you lay down, your work would have advanced slowly and you would not have lost heart." So the lad did what his father said, and in a short time the plot was cultivated.*

With each period of time we spend in our spiritual practice, we are clearing that one little spot of ground. We are moving, if imperceptibly, on our journey toward being who we really are, created to give and receive love.

## THE ANSWER IS YES

When Leonard Bernstein concluded the lectures at Harvard that became his wonderful book, *The Unanswered Question,* his final statement was, "I'm no longer quite sure what the question is, but I do know that the answer is yes."

Yes.

That is our answer to the call from the heart for a deep, nurturing connection with the Holy Other. The yielding of this center of consent may be a silent, slow development. Transformation may be gradual and pass unnoticed. It may be a slow permeation of the *Spiritus Creator* that marks no place or time.

The secret is to be able to want one thing, to seek one thing, to organize the resources of your life around a single end; and, slowly, surely, over time, you become one with that end. Your inner landscape becomes shaped by the single, central emphasis of your life—to become more and more conscious of the Divine's presence in your life and more and more able to give and to receive love.

Even though your progress is gradual and ongoing, you discover a wonderful thing—the confidence, peace, and certainty building in your life do not belong only to you. Because you create this sanctuary for God in your quiet time, you are able, amazingly enough, to allow others to borrow hope from you. You can become like a quarry from which people in pain and despair can take stones to start to build their lives anew. People can catch the atmosphere of hoping from you.

One way our lives—and the lives of others—change is by people opening new worlds to us that transform the quality of our consciousness. One thing people who spend time listening in quiet and speaking in prayer eventually come to experience for themselves and to be able to provide (on a good day!) for others, is a sense of poise and roominess. There are some people whose very presence—often as a result of many years of practicing a spiritual discipline—inspires a relaxation of inner tensions. To come in contact with them is to find your confidence restored by a general atmosphere of spaciousness and tranquillity. This quality is a profound result of moments of grace called into life, not by themselves but by a quickening Presence. This is the gift you hope to be able to give others out of your time of daily quiet and prayer.

## THE GIFT

And the gift to yourself?

There is an old story that resonates the value of practicing a spiritual discipline. The story goes like this:

> *A distinguished archaeologist spent several years working in the upper Amazon. He employed local men to help him with his work. Once the archaeologist and his workers had to walk a considerable distance to reach a new site. The party made very good progress for the first few days; but on the third morning, when it was time to start, the workers just sat without moving, looking very solemn and making no preparation to leave. The chief among the workers explained to the archeologist the problem: "They can't move any further until their souls have caught up to their bodies."*

That is what you are doing each day you practice daily sacred quiet time and prayer. You are living a commitment that is the very source of hope, peace, and serenity.

You are letting your soul catch up with your body.

In his eighty-fifth year, I had an opportunity during a talk with my father to see firsthand the kind of serenity and peace that years of practicing a daily spiritual discipline can bring. The impetus of the conversation was a kind of crisis of faith on my part.

(It is humbling to accept that I am always becoming more of who I can be . . . that I am never already there. It is reassuring, too, to accept that questions, and even doubts, will probably surface for the rest of my life, some in the very time of my daily quiet and prayer!)

The occasion was this: I was visiting my parents in their small retirement cottage on the banks of Possum Creek in Soddy-Daisy, Tennessee. For some time I found myself becoming more and more angry with God for the circumstances in which my father and mother found themselves in their old age. After all, hadn't Tommie preached for more than sixty years, given to the poor, worked for the needy (he started the first food pantry in that part of Tennessee back in the 1940s!)? Hadn't Rachel dedicated her life to being a preacher's wife, love and sweetness and kindness following her like the wake in a lake when a boat moves through? Hadn't they both sacrificed beyond measure . . . only now to end up at the end of their lives having to balance a payment for the electric heat against sending the check to AARP for this month's insurance? Where was justice in all this?

Finally, at a friend's suggestion, I decided to ask my father how he felt about the circumstances in which he and my mother lived. (Over the years I've come to see that one of the clearest ways God sends a message is through the words of some person who loves and cares for you.) We were sitting on the tiny screened-in porch on a slightly chilly late March day. Daddy was in his favorite chair—located where he could most easily see the goldfinches hovering around the feeder—and I sat in Mother's rocker.

"Daddy, I want to ask you something, and I hope it won't hurt your feelings." I rushed ahead before he could even speak, afraid I would lose my nerve.

"You and Mother have given your entire lives to God's work. You have preached and served under all kinds of conditions. You have given beyond your means to help others, financially and otherwise. Even now you give ten percent of the social security check you get every month to the church."

I swallowed and then hurried on.

"Now you're in your eighties, and you have to watch every penny. You and Mother do without things you could really use. How do you feel about this? Don't you think sometimes that God has let you down?"

My father's head snapped around, and he looked at me as if I had taken total leave of my senses. He didn't say a word for some seconds. Then, turning his gaze toward a spot on the left-hand side of the yard, he gestured with his long bony finger and spoke in as strong a voice as I had ever heard:

"Sister," he said, "you see that lily growing there?"

I looked and saw the milky white bloom of a single lily, the only flower so far that spring in the entire yard.

When he was sure I saw where he was pointing, my father said, without a waver, "God takes care of that lily. And God will take care of your Mother and me."

End of discussion. My father spoke, and I understood. What I had just heard was the certainty, assurance, and peace that came from a lifetime of practicing a daily spiritual discipline, through windstorms and through calm. A lifetime of connecting with God. A lifetime of prayer. A lifetime of love.

## R E F L E C T I O N

*What is the next chapter in your ongoing personal sacred story?*

### SACRED TASKS

Oh, how many people at different phases of my life have I borrowed hope from! Someone told me once, "Don't worry if you can't pray yourself. Just be sure you find someone to be with who can." I have followed that advice many times since. I feel sad; find someone who knows sadness but who also knows what it means to live through it and feel life stirring again. I am grieved; find someone who has hurt but whose loss has not darkened the heart. I have borrowed hope from them and have tried to be available so others can borrow hope from me.

TASK: Think back over your life. From whom have you ever borrowed hope? Who has borrowed hope from you? What were the events or feelings that brought you there?

We all remember the old saying, "A journey of a thousand miles begins with a single step." My first step in establishing a daily spiritual practice was to decide to spend five minutes reading something inspirational, saying the Lord's Prayer in my head while I sat quietly, and asking help for myself and others at the conclusion. From that tentative, wobbly, sometimes-did/some-times-didn't first step all else has followed.

TASK: What first step might you choose to begin a practice of daily quiet time and prayer? Or if you already have such a practice, what steps might you take to deepen and enlarge that experience?

*On the day I called, thou didst answer me:*
*My strength of soul thou didst increase.*

*—Psalm 138:3*

# END NOTES

## *Introduction*

PAGE xx
Elizabeth Johnson tells this story in her book *She Who Is,* p. 43.

## *Chapter One*

PAGE 27
*Dr. Robert Coles: The Spiritual Life of Children* has chapters on "The Face of God," "The Voice of God," "Visionary Moments," "Representations," and many other accounts of children's encounters with the Divine.

PAGE 30
*Verena Kast:* From *Joy, Inspiration, and Hope,* p. 45.

PAGE 32
*Kierkegaard*, cited in *The Transforming Moment,* James E. Loder, p. 5.

PAGE 33
*I, the highest and fiery power:* From the writings of Hildegard of Bingen, an extraordinary woman who lived in the twelfth century and who was a medical doctor; poet; artist; abbess; advisor to politicians, popes and kings; naturalist; authority on gems; linguist; missionary and preacher; founder of schools for girls; and a mystic. Quoted in *She Who Is,* Elizabeth A. Johnson, p. 124.
*Make a sanctuary for me:* Exodus 25: 8 (New International Version).

PAGE 34
*Those whose hearts were stirred:* Exodus 25:21–29 (Living Bible Version).
*Martin Buber:* cited in *She Who Is,* p. 75. We probably remember Buber best for his profound discussion of the distinction—and the relationship—between the *I* and the *Thou.*

## C h a p t e r   T w o

PAGE 42
*Fenced-off devotional patch:* From a book considered a classic, Evelyn
Underhill's *The Spiritual Life,* p. 24. Underhill, who lived from 1875 to
1941, was a prolific British writer and poet, radio commentator, and
magazine editor who, the *Encyclopedia Brittanica* says, "helped establish
mystical theology as a respectable discipline among contemporary
intellectuals."

PAGE 43
*As a person each of us:* From *The Creative Encounter,* pp. 19 and 23.

PAGE 44
*Paul Winter: Common Ground,* record album and cassette, 1978; com-
pact disc, 1989.

PAGE 45
*But I want first of all:* excerpt from *Gift from the Sea,* p. 17.

PAGE 46
*But there are techniques:* Ibid., p. 18.

PAGE 47
*Einstein's words:* From "Constructing a Theory: Einstein's Model," by
Gerald Horton, *The American Scholar,* Summer 1979, pp. 309–340.

PAGE 48
*To know that what is impenetrable:* from *What I Believe,* cited on the
Quintessential Quotations Website
(http://users.deltanet.com/~lumiere/quotes.htm).
*There is, after all:* from a letter to Queen Elizabeth of Belgium, 1936.
Cited in *Einstein: A Portrait,* p. 54.

PAGE 49
*The very nerve center of one's consent:* Mentioned in several of Thurman's
works. See *Disciplines of the Spirit,* p. 18; *The Creative Encounter,* p. 68.
*Ingathering:* from *Disciplines of the Spirit,* pp. 22, 23.

## C h a p t e r   T h r e e

PAGE 54
*I want to go home:* This first century B.C. Japanese poem is attributed to
Mei Shêng and Fu I.
*Gaston Bachelard:* From the Introduction, *The Poetics of Space,* pp.
xv–xxxix.

PAGE 56
*Amiri Baraka and W. E. B. DuBois:* From *The Spirituals and the Blues* by James H. Cone.

PAGE 58
*Only more so:* From a lecture presented to novitiates at Gethsemani Monastery in Louisville, Kentucky.
*City with windows of agate:* Isaiah 54.

PAGE 63
*The rain:* From *Raids on the Unspeakable*, pp. 9–10.

## Chapter Four

PAGE 74
*The shoes danced:* This fairy tale can be found in many collections. I have used the version quoted in *Women Who Run with the Wolves* by Clarissa Pinkola Estes, p. 216–219.

## Chapter Five

PAGE 81
*Work hard; It is good and fitting:* Eccelesiastes 9:10; Eccelesiastes 5:18–20. Pronoun changes are mine.

PAGE 83
*Christopher Alexander:* See *A Pattern Language* and *Timeless Way of Building.*

PAGE 85
*Poustinia:* A Russian word that means "desert" and is now used as the name of places specifically designed for solitude and silence. Catherine de Haeck Doherty pioneered the movement of developing poustinias. The story of the development of poustinias can be found in her book: *Poustinia: Christian Spirituality of the East for Western Man* (Notre Dame: Ave Maria Press, 1976).

PAGE 87
*Emily Whaley:* See *The New York Times,* June 19, 1998.

## Chapter Six

PAGE 92
*All references to Celtic way of praying:* From *The Celtic Way of Prayer* by Esther De Waal.

PAGE 93
*The embers:* De Waal, p. 47.

PAGE 94
*Francis de Sales:* All references to Francis' teachings on keeping a spiritual discipline are from his *Introduction to the Devout Life.*
*Marie:* In *Introduction to the Devout Life* Francis used the name "Philomena," which means "soul searching for God," instead of his cousin's name, Marie.

PAGE 101
*John Lewis:* From *How I Pray,* pp. 84–87.

PAGE 102
*Richard Foster:* From *How I Pray,* pp. 30–38.

## Chapter Seven

PAGE 109
*Anne Truitt:* From *Daybook: The Journal of an Artist,* p. 130.

PAGE 113
*Dame Julian:* From *Meditations with Julian of Norwich,* pp. 25 and 37.
*Brother Lawrence:* See *The Practice of the Presence of God.*

PAGE 116
*A journal:* Anne Broyles' *Journaling: A Spiritual Journey* and Christina Baldwin's *Life's Companion: Journal Writing as a Spiritual Quest* are excellent sources for ideas.

PAGE 117
*William Stafford:* Adapted from *Writing the Australian Crawl: Views on the Writer's Vocation,* p. 17.

PAGE 119
*Two Obituaries:* See *The New York Times,* April 3, 1998 and *The New York Times,* March 26, 1998.
*Joseph Campbell:* Cited in *Life's Companion: Journal Writing as a Spiritual Quest,* p. 52.

## Chapter Eight

PAGE 124
*If it were just a matter:* Cited in *Parabola,* Summer 1990, p. 67.

PAGE 125
*Anthony Bloom:* From *Beginning to Pray,* pp. 92-94.
*Sacrament of pause:* a phrase attributed to Howard Thurman.

PAGE 127
*John Main:* From *The Way of Unknowing,* p. ix.

PAGE 128
*Centering Prayer:* Adapted from a pamphlet "Finding Peace at the Center," by Fr. M. Basil Pennington, OCSO. See also *Centering Prayer in Daily Life and Ministry* by Gustave Reininger.

PAGE 129
*Eknath Easwaran:* From *Meditation: An Eight-Point Program,* pp. 29–56.

PAGE 132–133
*Peter Brook and Gertrude Stein:* From *Parabola,* Summer 1988, pp. 57–59; 80–81.

PAGE 134
*Your bodily wits:* Cited in Michael Casey's *Toward God: The Ancient Wisdom of Western Prayer,* p. 102.

*C h a p t e r   N i n e*

PAGE 141
*Thomas Merton's prayer:* From *Thoughts in Solitude,* p. 89.

PAGE 142
*George Gallup, High Star, Martin Marty, Carole Mu'Min:* From *How I Pray,* pp. 39, 64, 88, 99.

PAGE 143
*A survey:* Discussed in the book *Toxic Faith* by Steve Arterbum and Jack Felton.

PAGE 145
*Wichita, Kansas:* See "Richard J. Foster," *How I Pray,* p. 35. *William Temple:* Cited in *The Workbook of Living Prayer* by Maxie Dunnam, p. 80.

PAGE 146
*San Francisco General Hospital:* Numerous sources cite statistics on the study of prayer and describe this study on the effectiveness of prayer specifically. See Pulitzer Prize-winning and Tony award-winning playwright Marsha Norman's article in *Self* magazine called "Say Amen to Somebody"; Dr. Dean Ornish's *Program for Reversing Heart Disease; USA Today's* article, December 21, 1993, "The Healing Power of Prayer," *Reader's Digest,* "Does Prayer Heal?," March 1996; and *Lotus* magazine's interview with Larry Dossey, M.D. in the anniversary issue of 1995.

PAGE 147
*Ann and Barry Ulanov:* Their book *Primary Speech: A Psychology of Prayer* teaches and inspires me. Many of the varieties of ways in which prayers are answered came to my mind after reading this book.

PAGE 148
*Sense of causality:* A statement by Ann and Barry Ulanov.

PAGE 150
*I gave myself plenty of time:* From Howard Thurman's book, *Disciplines of the Spirit,* p. 100.
*Other side of the coin:* This ancient story is told in Roberta Bondi's book, *To Pray and to Love,* p. 126.

PAGE 152
*Four things:* See Maxie Dunnam's *The Workbook of Living Prayer,* one of the most accessible and inspiring books on prayer I have read, for discussion of the first three of these four things.

## Chapter Ten

PAGE 162
*Martin Buber:* From *Spiritual Illuminations,* edited by Peg Streep, p. 99.

PAGE 164
*Movie:* The film is titled *The Razor's Edge.*

## Chapter Eleven

PAGE 169
*God did not say:* From *Meditations with Julian of Norwich,* p. 115.
*Just so the wonder:* From *A Retreat with Job & Julian of Norwich: Trusting That All Will Be Well,* p. 80.

PAGE 170
*Hildegard:* See references to Hildegard in Elizabeth Johnson's *She Who Is,* pp. 124, 127, 128.

PAGE 171
*Husband:* For a full account of this event, see the book I wrote called *Seven Choices: Taking the Steps to New Life After Losing Someone You Love.*

PAGE 173
*Elie Wiesel:* See *The New York Times,* October 2, 1997.

PAGE 174
*Power-with:* For an inspiring discussion of this concept see Elizabeth Johnson's *She Who Is.*

PAGE 175
*Rabbi Marc Gellman and Father Tom Hartman:* Quoted in *Self* magazine, September 1997, p. 68.

*Chapter Twelve*

PAGE 178
*Blacksmith story:* Told in *Parabola,* Summer 1988, p. 120.

PAGE 180
*Dr. Elizabeth Johnson:* From *She Who Is,* pp. 124–127.

PAGE 182
*Neither death:* Paul writing to friends in Romans 8:38–39

PAGE 183
*A man had a plot of land:* Quoted in *To Pray & To Love,* p. 57.

PAGE 184
*Leonard Bernstein:* From *The Unanswered Question,* p. 425.

PAGE 185
*A distinguished archaeologist:* Story included in *The Fire of Silence and Stillness,* p. 126.

# BIBLIOGRAPHY

Armstrong, Karen. *A History of God*. New York: Ballantine Books, 1994.

Bachelard, Gaston. *The Poetics of Space*. Boston, MA: Beacon Press, 1994.

Baldwin, Christina. *Life's Companion: Journal Writing as a Spiritual Quest*. New York: Bantam, 1991.

Bloom, Anthony. *Beginning to Pray*. Ramsey, NJ: Paulist Press, 1970.

Bondi, Roberta. *To Pray and to Love*. Minneapolis, MN: Augsburg Fortress, 1991.

Broyles, Anne. *Journaling: A Spirit Journey*. Nashville, TN: The Upper Room, 1988.

Casey, Michael. *Toward God: The Ancient Wisdom of Western Prayer*. Liguori, MO: Triumph Books, 1996.

Castelli, Jim. *How I Pray*. New York: Ballantine Books, 1994.

Coles, Robert. *The Spiritual Life of Children*. Boston, MA: Houghton Mifflin Company, 1990.

De Sales, Francis. *Introduction to the Devout Life*. New York: Doubleday, 1989.

De Waal, Esther. *The Celtic Way of Prayer*. New York: Doubleday, 1997.

Doyle, Brendan. *Julian of Norwich*. Santa Fe, NM: Bear & Company, Inc., 1983.

Dunnam, Maxie. *The Workbook of Living Prayer*. Nashville, TN: The Upper Room, 1974.

Dunne, John S. *Love's Mind: An Essay on Contemplative Life*. Notre Dame, IN: University of Notre Dame Press, 1993.

Easwaran, Eknath. *Meditation: An Eight-Point Program*. Petaluma, CA: Nilgiri Press, 1993.

Estes, Clarissa Pinkola. *Women Who Run with the Wolves*. New York: Ballantine Books, 1992.

Foster, Richard. *Celebration of Discipline: The Path to Spiritual Growth.* New York: Harper & Row, 1978.

Gallup, George H. and Timothy Jones. *The Saints Among Us.* Harrisburg, PA: Morehouse Publishing, 1992.

Harris, Paul. *The Fire of Silence and Stillness.* Springfield, IL: Templegate Publishers, 1995.

Higgins, John J. *Thomas Merton on Prayer.* New York: Doubleday, 1975.

Holton, Gerald. "Einstein's Model," *The American Scholar,* Summer 1979, pp. 309–339.

Johnson, Elizabeth A. *She Who Is.* New York: The Crossroad Publishing Company, 1992.

Juliana of Norwich. *Revelations of Divine Love.* New York: Image Books, 1977.

Kast, Verena. *Joy, Inspiration, and Hope.* College Station, TX: The Texas A&M University Press, 1991.

Lawrence, Brother. *The Practice of the Presence of God.* White Plains, NY Peter Pauper Press, Inc.

Leubering, Carol. *Job & Julian of Norwich.* Cincinnati, OH: St. Anthony Messenger, 1995.

Lindbergh, Anne Morrow. *Gift from the Sea.* New York: Pantheon Books, 1975.

Loder, James. *The Transforming Moment.* Colorado Springs, CO: Helmers & Howard, Publishers, Inc., 1989.

Main, John. *The Way of Unknowing.* New York: The Crossroad Publishing Company, 1989.

Merton, Thomas. *Thoughts in Solitude.* Boston, MA: Shambhala Publications, Inc., 1993.

Metzger, Deena. *Writing for Your Life.* San Francisco, CA: Harper San Francisco, 1992.

Neeld, Elizabeth Harper. *Seven Choices: Taking the Steps to New Life After Losing Someone You Love.* Third Edition, Revised. Houston, TX: Center-point Press, 1997.

Newman, Barbara. *Sister of Wisdom.* Berkeley, CA: University of California Press, 1987.

Ornish, Dean. *Dr. Dean Ornish's Program for Reversing Heart Disease.* New York: Ballantine Books, 1990.

Reininger, Gustave. *Centering Prayer in Daily Life and Ministry.* New York: The Continuum Publishing Company, 1998.

Stafford, William. *Writing the Australian Crawl: Views on the Writer's Vocation.* Ann Arbor, MI: The University of Michigan Press, 1978.

Streep, Peg. *Spiritual Illuminations.* New York: Viking Studio Books, 1992.

Thurman, Howard. *The Centering Moment.* Richmond, IN: Friends United Press, 1990.

Thurman, Howard. *The Creative Encounter.* Richmond, IN: Friends United Press, 1972.

Thurman, Howard. *Deep Is the Hunger.* Richmond, IN: Friends United Press, 1990.

Thurman, Howard. *Disciplines of the Spirit.* Richmond, IN: Friends United Press, 1987.

Truitt, Anne. *Daybook: The Journal of an Artist.* New York: Penguin Books, 1985.

Ulanov, Ann & Barry. *Primary Speech: A Psychology of Prayer.* Atlanta, GA: John Knox Press, 1982.

Underhill, Evelyn. *The Spiritual Life.* Harrisburg, PA: Morehouse Publishing, 1994.

Winokur, Mark. *Einstein: A Portrait.* Corte Madera, CA: Pomegranate Artbooks, 1984.

# ABOUT THE AUTHOR

Elizabeth Harper Neeld, Ph.D. is an independent scholar with a doctorate in 18th century literature. She is the author/editor of sixteen books, including *Seven Choices: Taking the Steps to New Life after Losing Someone You Love.* She is a corporate consultant to Fortune 500 companies in the field of change management. She also teaches spiritual seminars and retreats, and is the lay-director of the Women's Retreat Ministry at the largest United Methodist Church in America, located in Houston, Texas. She resides in Austin, Texas. If you would like to bring a "sacred quiet time prayer" seminar to your community or church organization, please contact the author at: P.O. Box 200255418, Austin, TX 78720; e-mail: cppaustin.aol.com.

# PERMISSIONS